THE ULTIMAT   F

SNAKES

AND REPTILES

Discover the amazing world of snakes, crocodiles, lizards and turtles, with over 700 photographs and illustrations

Barbara Taylor & Mark O'Shea

ARMADILLO

CONTENTS

Introducing Reptiles 6

LIZARDS 128

TURTLES 188

Introducing Reptiles

Reptiles are animals such as lizards, snakes, turtles and crocodiles. These prehistoric survivors have lived on Earth for hundreds of millions of years. Most of the reptiles that lived long ago, such as the dinosaurs, are now extinct but there are still more than 7,000 different species roaming around the world today.

All reptiles have a bony skeleton, breathe through lungs and are covered by a scaly or leathery skin, which keeps their bodies from drying out. They rely on their surroundings for warmth and most of them live in warmer places on land, such as rainforests and deserts. Some live in rivers, lakes and swamps, while a few swim through the oceans.

The scales of snakes and lizards overlap to form a protective sheet that covers the whole body. Turtles, tortoises and crocodilians usually have rows of scales, called scutes.

Each reptile group has its own distinctive characteristics. The largest group is the lizards, with almost 4,000 species. A typical lizard has a small, slim body, four well-developed legs that stick out to the side, sharp claws and a long tail. Some lizards can break off their tail to help them escape predators. A new tail eventually grows to replace the old one. Most lizards have a mouthful of small sharp teeth and are swift, agile hunters of small animals.

The second largest reptile group is the snakes. The 2,700 species of snakes are unusual reptiles with no legs, eyelids or external ears. Their forked tongue tastes and smells the air. All snakes are carnivores, killing animals by biting them with venomous fangs or coiling around their bodies and squeezing hard to suffocate them.

A snake's jaws are very stretchy and open extremely wide to allow them to swallow large meals.

The crocodilian reptile group of some 22 species of crocodiles, alligators, caimans and gharials does not contain any venomous kinds but some crocodilians are fearsome predators because of their size. The biggest crocodilian, a large saltwater crocodile, or 'saltie', reaches lengths of up to 6.7m/22ft. The longest snake, the reticulated python, can grow slightly longer than this, but cannot match a 'saltie' for sheer aggression, power and speed. The prehistoric lizard, Megalania, grew to the same size as a 'saltie' but the biggest lizard alive today, the Komodo Dragon, grows no longer than 3m/10ft or so. The Komodo dragon is the only living lizard to threaten people, but big crocodilians and snakes (especially 300 of the most venomous snakes), are also capable of killing people. Surprisingly, most crocodilians and snakes are timid creatures and avoid human beings wherever possible.

Alligators move regularly in and out of the water searching for food. When they are not on the hunt for food they can be found basking in the sun.

The 300 species of chelonians include tortoises and terrapins as well as turtles. Most chelonians are harmless, although snapping turtles have vile tempers and jaws strong enough to bite through peoples' fingers! Chelonians are protected by their strong bony shells. Sea and freshwater species tend to have flatter, lighter shells to make them more streamlined for swimming. Land species are more likely to have high domed shells to protect them from predators. The biggest shells of all belong to the giant tortoises of the Galapagos and Aldabra Islands.

All chelonians, even the sea turtles, lay their waterproof eggs on land and don't look after their young. Most other reptiles also lay eggs on land, but a few lizards and snakes give birth to live young. This allows them to survive in colder climates, because the young can develop in the warmth of their mother's body. There is hardly any parental care in lizards and snakes, but mother crocodilians are responsible parents, helping their eggs to hatch and guarding their tiny young for a few weeks.

Sea turtles use their strong flippers to 'fly' underwater. Some of them are very fast swimmers, reaching speeds of up to 29kph/18mph.

Both young and old reptiles need our help if they are to survive. People kill these remarkable animals for their meat, skin and other body parts. They also destroy their habitats, collect their eggs or sell young wild reptiles as pets. Many reptiles, such as snakes, are killed because people think they are more dangerous than they really are. Conservation measures such as captive breeding, stopping illegal trade, education and protection in reserves are essential if a variety of reptiles are to share our future world.

SNAKES

Coiled motionless around tree branches or
slithering silently through the under-
growth, snakes are the most secretive and
feared of all the reptiles. Yet fewer than
a quarter of all snakes are venomous, and
they rarely attack people unless provoked.
The smallest snakes are as thin as a pencil,
while the largest can be 30cm/12in wide.
All sizes of snake are fascinating, from
hooded cobras and buzzing rattlesnakes to
bright coral snakes and amazing adders.

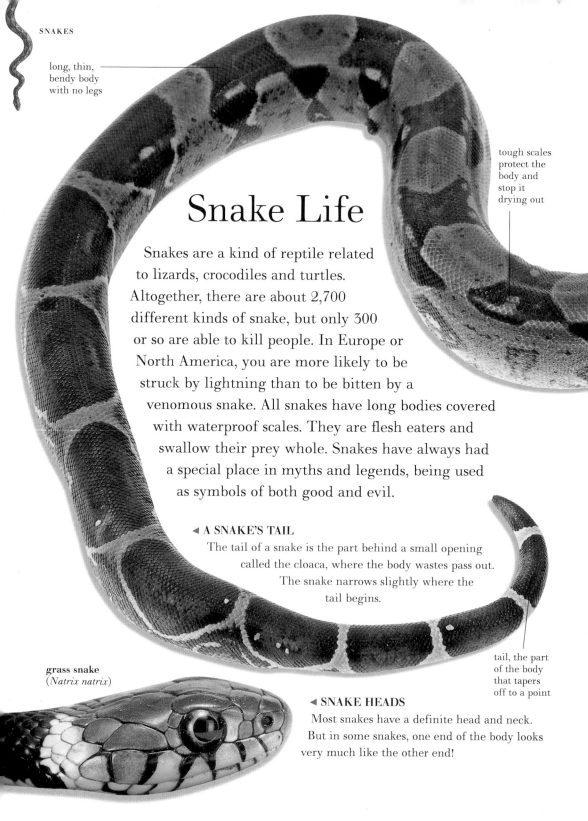

long, thin, bendy body with no legs

tough scales protect the body and stop it drying out

Snake Life

Snakes are a kind of reptile related to lizards, crocodiles and turtles. Altogether, there are about 2,700 different kinds of snake, but only 300 or so are able to kill people. In Europe or North America, you are more likely to be struck by lightning than to be bitten by a venomous snake. All snakes have long bodies covered with waterproof scales. They are flesh eaters and swallow their prey whole. Snakes have always had a special place in myths and legends, being used as symbols of both good and evil.

◄ A SNAKE'S TAIL
The tail of a snake is the part behind a small opening called the cloaca, where the body wastes pass out. The snake narrows slightly where the tail begins.

tail, the part of the body that tapers off to a point

grass snake
(*Natrix natrix*)

◄ SNAKE HEADS
Most snakes have a definite head and neck. But in some snakes, one end of the body looks very much like the other end!

◄ FORKED TONGUES

Snakes and some lizards have forked tongues. A snake flicks its tongue to taste and smell the air. This gives the snake a picture of what is around it. A snake does this every few seconds if it is hunting or if there is any danger nearby.

rattlesnake
(*Crotalus*)

Colombian rainbow boa
(*Epicrates cenchria maurus*)

▲ SCALY SKIN

A covering of tough, dry scales grows out of a snake's skin. The scales usually hide the skin. After a big meal, the scaly skin stretches so that the skin becomes visible between the scales. A snake's scales protect its body while allowing it to stretch, coil and bend. The scales may be either rough or smooth.

red-tailed boa
(*Boa constrictor*)

Did you know? Snakes never feel slimy to the touch.

Did you know? A boa squeezes its prey to death in its coils.

Medusa

An ancient Greek myth tells of Medusa, a monster with snakes for hair. Anyone who looked at her was turned to stone. Perseus managed to avoid this fate by using his polished shield to look only at the monster's reflection. He cut off Medusa's head and carried it home, dripping with blood. As each drop touched the earth, it turned into a snake.

eye has no eyelid

forked tongue

Shapes and Sizes

Can you imagine a snake as tall as a three-storey house? The reticulated python is this big. The biggest snakes' bodies measure nearly 1m (3ft) in circumference. Other snakes are as thin as a pencil and small enough to fit into the palm of your hand. Snakes also have different shapes to suit their environments. Sea snakes, for example, have flat bodies and tails like oars to help them push against the water and move forwards.

▼ **THICK AND THIN**

Vipers mostly have thick bodies with much thinner, short tails. The bags of venom on either side of a viper's head take up a lot of space, so the head is quite large.

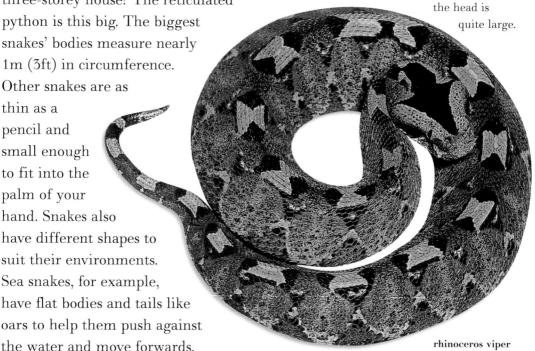

rhinoceros viper
(*Bitis nasicornis*)

◄ **LONG AND THIN**

A tree snake's long, thin shape helps it to slide along leaves and branches. Even its head is long, pointed and very light so that it does not weigh the snake down as it reaches for the next branch.

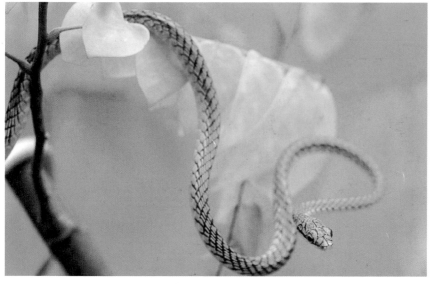

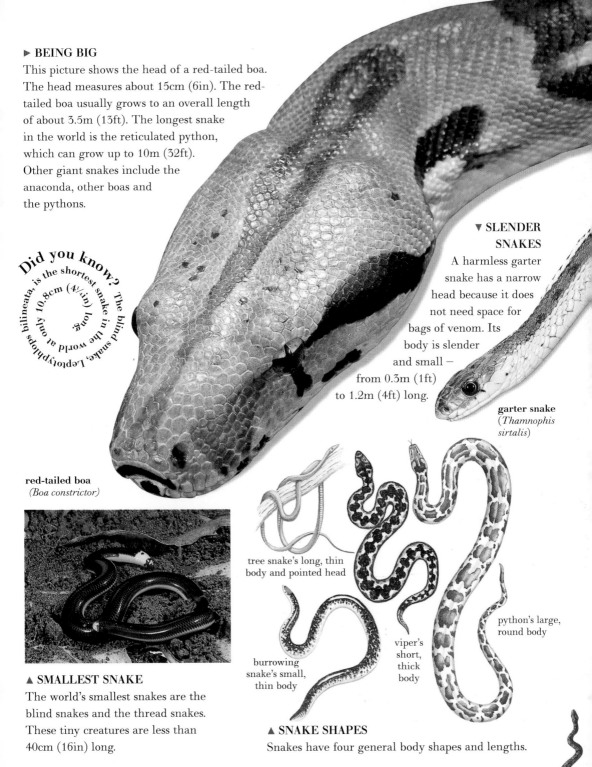

► BEING BIG

This picture shows the head of a red-tailed boa. The head measures about 15cm (6in). The red-tailed boa usually grows to an overall length of about 3.5m (13ft). The longest snake in the world is the reticulated python, which can grow up to 10m (32ft). Other giant snakes include the anaconda, other boas and the pythons.

Did you know?

The blind snake, Leptotyphlops bilineata, is the shortest snake in the world at only 10.8cm (4¼in) long.

▼ SLENDER SNAKES

A harmless garter snake has a narrow head because it does not need space for bags of venom. Its body is slender and small — from 0.3m (1ft) to 1.2m (4ft) long.

garter snake
(*Thamnophis sirtalis*)

red-tailed boa
(*Boa constrictor*)

tree snake's long, thin body and pointed head

python's large, round body

viper's short, thick body

burrowing snake's small, thin body

▲ SMALLEST SNAKE

The world's smallest snakes are the blind snakes and the thread snakes. These tiny creatures are less than 40cm (16in) long.

▲ SNAKE SHAPES

Snakes have four general body shapes and lengths.

egg-eating
snake
(*Dasypeltis
fasciata*)

◄ STRETCHY STOMACH
Luckily, the throat and gut of the egg-eating
snake are so elastic that its thin body
can stretch enough
to swallow a whole
egg. Muscles in the
throat and first part of
the gut help force food
down into the stomach.

How Snakes Work

A snake has a stretched-out inside to match
its long, thin outside. The backbone extends
along the whole body with hundreds of ribs joined
to it. There is not much room for organs such as the
heart, lungs, kidneys and liver, so these organs are thin
shapes to fit inside the snake's body. Many snakes have
only one lung. The stomach and gut are stretchy so that
they can hold large meals. When a snake swallows big
prey, it pushes the opening of the windpipe up from
the floor of the mouth in order to keep breathing.
Snakes are cold-blooded, which means that their
body temperature is the same as their surroundings.

right lung is
very long and
thin and does
the work of
two lungs

liver is very
long and thin

flexible tail bone,
which extends
from the back
bone

▼ INSIDE A SNAKE
This diagram shows
the inside of a male
snake. The organs are
arranged to fit the
snake's long shape. In
most species, paired
organs, such as the
kidneys, are the
same size and
placed opposite
each other.

▲ COLD-BLOODED CREATURE
Like all snakes, the banded rattlesnake is cold-blooded.

rectum through
which waste is
passed to the cloaca

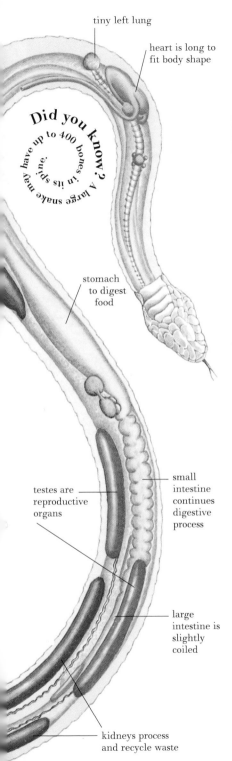

tiny left lung

heart is long to
fit body shape

Did you know?
A large snake may have up to 400 bones in its spine.

stomach
to digest
food

testes are
reproductive
organs

small
intestine
continues
digestive
process

large
intestine is
slightly
coiled

kidneys process
and recycle waste

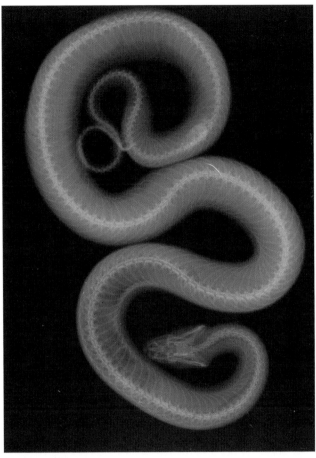

▲ SNAKE BONES

This X-ray of a grass snake shows the delicate bones that
make up its skeleton. There are no arm, leg, shoulder or hip
bones. The snake's ribs do not extend into the tail.

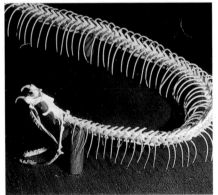

◄ SKELETON

A snake's skeleton
is made up of a
skull and a long
backbone with ribs
arching out from
it. The free ends of
the ribs are linked
by muscles.

A Scaly Skin

▼ HORNED SNAKE

As its name suggests, the European nose-horned viper has a strange horn on its nose. The horn is made up of small scales that lie over a bony or fleshy lump sticking out at the end of the nose.

A snake's scales are extra-thick pieces of skin. Like a hard shell, the scales protect the snake from knocks and scrapes as it moves. They also allow the skin to stretch when the snake moves or feeds. Scales are usually made of a horny substance, called keratin. Every part of a snake's body is covered by a layer of scales, including the eyes. The clear, bubble-like scale that protects each eye is called a brille or spectacle.

nose-horned viper
(*Vipera ammodytes*)

▼ SCUTES

Most snakes have a row of broad scales, called scutes, underneath their bodies. The scutes go across a snake's body from side to side, and end where the tail starts. Scutes help snakes to grip the ground.

▼ WARNING RATTLE

The rattlesnake has a number of hollow tail-tips that make a buzzing sound when shaken. The snake uses this sound to warn enemies. When it sheds its skin, a section at the end of the tail is left, adding another piece to the rattle.

rattlesnake's rattle

corn snake's scutes

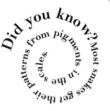

▶ SKIN SCALES

The scales of a snake grow out of the top layer of the skin, called the epidermis. There are different kinds of scales. Keeled scales may help snakes to grip surfaces, or break up a snake's outline for camouflage. Smooth scales make it easier for the snake to squeeze through tight spaces.

Look closely at the rough scales of the puff adder (left) and you will see a raised ridge, or keel, sticking up in the middle of each one.

corn snake's scales

The wart snake (right) uses its scales to grip its food. Its rough scales help the snake to keep a firm hold on slippery fish until it can swallow them. The snake's scales do not overlap.

The green scales and stretched blue skin (left) belong to a boa. These smooth scales help the boa to slide over leafy branches. Burrowing snakes have smooth scales so that they can slip through soil.

Eternal Youth

A poem written in the Middle East about 3,700 years ago tells a story about why snakes can shed their skins. The hero of the poem is Gilgamesh (shown here holding a captured lion). He finds a magic plant that will make a person young again. While he is washing at a pool, a snake eats the plant. Since then, snakes have been able to shed their skins and become young again. But people have never found the plant — which is why they always grow old and die.

1 In the days before its skin peels, a snake is bad-tempered and sluggish, and it is dull in appearance. Its eyes turn cloudy as their coverings loosen. About a day before shedding, the eyes clear.

Focus on New Skin

About six times a year, an adult snake wriggles out of its old, tight skin to reveal a new, shiny skin underneath. Snakes shed their worn-out skin and scales in one piece. This process is called shedding or sloughing. Snakes only shed when a new layer of skin and scales has grown underneath the old skin. Adult snakes do this up to about six times a year.

2 The paper-thin layer of outer skin and scales first starts to peel away around the mouth. The snake rubs its jaws and chin against rocks or rough bark, and crawls through plants. This helps to push off the loose layer of skin.

Did you know? A baby snake may shed its skin when it is only a few days old

3 The outer layer of skin gradually peels back from the head over the rest of the body. The snake slides out of its old skin, which comes off inside-out. It is rather like taking hold of a long sock at the top and peeling it down over your leg and foot!

Did you know? Female snakes often shed their skin just before giving birth.

4 A snake usually takes several hours to shed its whole skin. The old skin is moist and supple soon after shedding, but gradually dries out to become crinkly and rather brittle. The discarded skin is a copy of the snake's scale pattern. It is very delicate, and if you hold it up to the light, it is almost see-through.

5 A shed skin is longer than the snake itself. This is because the skin stretches as the snake wriggles free.

19

Snakes on the Move

For animals without legs, snakes move around very well. They can glide over or under the ground, climb trees and swim through water. A few snakes can even parachute through the air. Snakes are not speedy – most move at about 3kph (2mph). Their bendy backbones give them a wavy movement. They push themselves along using muscles joined to their ribs. The scales on their skin also grip surfaces to help with movement.

Did you know? A person can walk faster than a snake can move.

▶ **S-SHAPED MOVER**

Most snakes move in an S-shaped path, pushing the side curves of their bodies backwards against the surface they are moving on or through. The muscular waves of the snake's body hit surrounding objects and the whole body is pushed forward from there.

▼ **CONCERTINA SNAKE**

The green whip snake moves with an action rather like a concertina (see the diagram on the facing page). A concertina is played by squeezing it forwards and backwards.

▲ **SWIMMING SNAKE**

The banded sea snake's stripes stand out as it glides through the water. Snakes swim using S-shaped movements. A sea snake's tail is flattened from side to side to give it extra power, like the oar on a row boat.

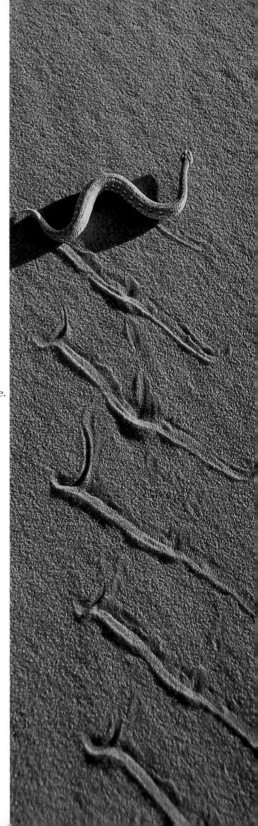

corn snake
(Elaphe guttata)

Did you know? The fastest land snake is the black mamba, moving at up to 11kph (7mph).

▶ **SIDEWINDING**
The way snakes that live on loose sand move along is called sidewinding. The snake anchors its head and tail in the sand and throws the middle part of its body sideways.

▼ **HOW SNAKES MOVE**
Most land snakes move in four different ways, depending on the type of terrain they are crossing and the type of snake.

1 S-shaped movement: the snake wriggles from side to side.

2 Concertina movement: the snake pulls one half of its body along first, then the other half.

3 Sidewinding movement: the snake throws the middle part of its body forwards, keeping the head and tail on the ground.

4 Caterpillar movement: the snake uses its belly scutes to pull itself along in a straight line.

▲ EYESIGHT
Snakes have no eyelids to cover their eyes. Eyesight varies in snakes, but those with the best eyesight are tree snakes, such as this green mamba, and day hunters such as garter snakes.

Snake Senses

To find prey and avoid enemies, snakes rely more on their senses of smell, taste and touch than on sight and hearing. Snakes have no ears, but they do have one earbone joined at the jaw. The lower jaw picks up sound vibrations moving through the ground. As well as ordinary senses, snakes also have some special ones. They are one of the few animals that taste and smell with their tongues.

▲ NIGHT HUNTER
The horned viper's eyes open wide at night (*above*). During the day, its pupils close to narrow slits (*below*).

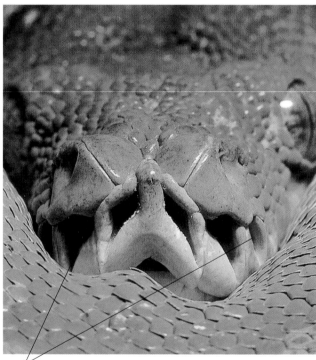

heat pits

▲ SENSING HEAT
The green tree python senses heat given off by its prey through pits on the sides of its face. These heat sensors are lined with nerves. They allow a snake to find and kill prey even in total darkness.

◄ THE FORKED TONGUE

When a snake wants to investigate its surroundings, it flicks its tongue to taste the air. The forked tongue picks up tiny chemical particles of scent.

▲ HEARING

As it has no ears, the cobra cannot hear the music played by the snake charmer. It follows the movements of the pipe, which resemble a snake, and rises up as it prepares to defend itself.

► JACOBSON'S ORGAN

As a snake draws its tongue back into its mouth, it presses the forked tip into the two openings of the Jacobson's organ. This organ is in the roof of the mouth and it analyses tastes and smells.

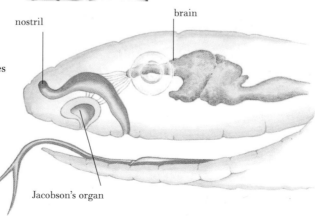

nostril

brain

Jacobson's organ

Food and Hunting

Snakes eat different foods and hunt in different ways depending on their size, their species and where they live. Some snakes eat a wide variety of food, while others have a more specialized diet. A snake has to make the most of each meal because it moves fairly slowly and does not get the chance to catch prey very often. A snake's body works at a slow rate so it can go for months without eating.

rat snake
(*Elaphe*)

▲ TREE HUNTERS
A rat snake grasps a baby bluebird in its jaws and begins the process of digestion. Rat snakes often slither up trees in search of baby birds, eggs or squirrels.

▲ FISHY FOOD
The tentacled snake lives on fish. It probably hides among plants in the water and grabs fish as they swim past.

▼ TRICKY LURE
The Australasian death adder's bright tail tip looks like a worm. The adder wriggles the 'worm' to lure lizards, birds and small mammals to come within its range.

◄ **EGG-EATERS**
The African egg-eater snake checks an egg with its tongue to make sure it is fresh. Then it swallows the egg whole. It uses the pointed ends of the bones in its backbone to crack the eggshell. It eats the egg and coughs up the crushed shell.

► **SURPRISE ATTACK**
Lunch for this gaboon viper is a mouse! The gaboon viper hides among dry leaves on the forest floor. Its pattern and markings make it very difficult to spot. It waits for a small animal to pass by, then grabs hold of its prey in a surprise attack. Many other snakes that hunt by day also ambush their prey.

Did you know? Sometimes a snake coughs up its prey – alive!

smooth snake
(*Coronella austriaca*)

◄ **SNAKE EATS SNAKE**
This smooth snake is eating an asp viper. The viper fits neatly inside the body of the smooth snake. This makes it easier to swallow than animals that are different shapes.

Teeth and Jaws

Most snakes have short, sharp teeth that are good for gripping and holding prey, but not for chewing it into smaller pieces. The teeth are not very strong, and often get broken, so they are continually being replaced. Venomous snakes also have some larger teeth called fangs. When the snake bites, venom flows down the fangs to paralyse the prey and break down its body. All snakes swallow their prey head-first and whole. Special loose jaws allow the snake to open its mouth very wide.

▼ **BACK FANGS**
A few venomous snakes have fangs at the back of their mouths. This African boomslang is digging its fangs hard into a chameleon's flesh to get enough venom inside.

viper skull

movable fangs

▲ **OPEN WIDE**
An eyelash viper opens its mouth as wide as possible to scare an enemy. Its fangs are folded back against the roof of the mouth. When it attacks, the fangs swing forwards.

▲ **FOLDING FANGS**
Vipers and elapid snakes have fangs at the front of the mouth. A viper's long fangs can fold back. When it strikes, the fangs swing forward to stick out in front of the mouth.

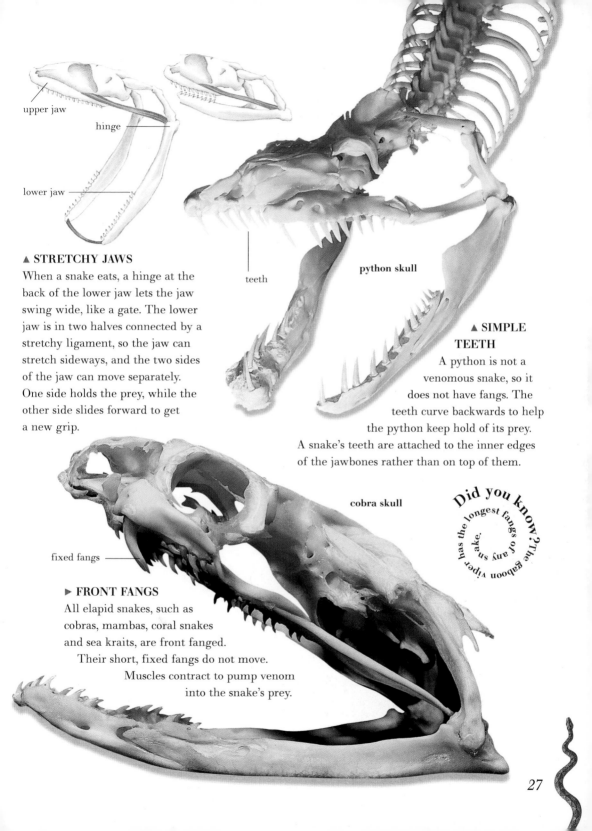

upper jaw

hinge

lower jaw

▲ STRETCHY JAWS

When a snake eats, a hinge at the back of the lower jaw lets the jaw swing wide, like a gate. The lower jaw is in two halves connected by a stretchy ligament, so the jaw can stretch sideways, and the two sides of the jaw can move separately. One side holds the prey, while the other side slides forward to get a new grip.

teeth

python skull

▲ SIMPLE TEETH

A python is not a venomous snake, so it does not have fangs. The teeth curve backwards to help the python keep hold of its prey. A snake's teeth are attached to the inner edges of the jawbones rather than on top of them.

cobra skull

Did you know? The gaboon viper has the longest fangs of any snake.

fixed fangs

► FRONT FANGS

All elapid snakes, such as cobras, mambas, coral snakes and sea kraits, are front fanged. Their short, fixed fangs do not move. Muscles contract to pump venom into the snake's prey.

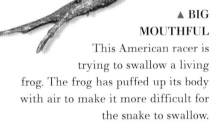

Stranglers and Poisoners

Most snakes kill their prey before eating it. Snakes kill by using venom or by squeezing their prey to death. Snakes that squeeze, called constrictors, stop their prey from breathing. Victims die from suffocation or shock. To swallow living or dead prey, a snake opens its jaws wide. Lots of slimy saliva helps the meal to slide down. After eating, a snake yawns widely to put its jaws back into place. Digestion can take several days, or even weeks.

American racer
(*Coluber constrictor*)

▲ BIG MOUTHFUL
This American racer is trying to swallow a living frog. The frog has puffed up its body with air to make it more difficult for the snake to swallow.

▲ AT FULL STRETCH
This fer-de-lance snake is at full stretch to swallow its huge meal. It is a large pit viper that kills with venom.

▲ SWALLOWING A MEAL
The copperhead, a venomous snake from North America, holds on to a dead mouse.

▲ KILLING TIME

A crocodile is slowly squeezed to death by a rock python. The time it takes for a constricting snake to kill its prey depends on the size of the prey and how strong it is.

spotted python
(*Liasis maculosus*)

► COILED KILLER

The spotted python sinks its teeth into its victim. It throws coils around the victim's body, and tightens its grip until the animal cannot breathe.

▲ HEAD-FIRST

A whiptail wallaby's legs disappear inside a carpet python's body. Snakes usually try to swallow their prey head-first so that legs, wings or scales fold back. This helps the victim to slide into the snake's stomach more easily.

▼ BREATHING TUBE

An African python shows its breathing tube. As the snake eats, the windpipe moves to the front of the mouth so that air can get to and from the lungs.

1 Rat snakes feed on rats, mice, voles, lizards, birds and eggs. Many of them hunt at night. They are good climbers and can even go up trees with smooth bark and no branches. Rat snakes find their prey by following a scent trail or waiting to ambush an animal.

Focus on Lunch!

This rat snake is using its strong coils to kill a vole. Rodents, such as voles and rats, are a rat snake's preferred food. With the vole held tightly in its teeth, the snake coils around its body. It squeezes hard to stop the vole breathing. When the vole is dead, the rat snake swallows its meal head-first.

2 When the rat snake is near enough to its prey, it strikes quickly. Its sharp teeth sink into the victim's body to stop it running or flying away. The snake then loops its coils around the victim as fast as possible, before the animal can bite or scratch to defend itself.

3 Each time the vole breathes out, the rat snake squeezes harder around its rib cage to stop the vole breathing in again. Breathing becomes more difficult and soon the victim dies from suffocation.

4 Once the victim is dead, the rat snake loosens its coils and begins the process of swallowing. It unhinges its jaws and 'walks' its mouth over its meal. The loose lower jaw stretches sideways to fit around the shape of the dead prey.

5 The rat snake swallows its meal head-first. As the vole moves down the snake's throat, its legs fold back against the sides of its body. The way the fur lies makes the vole easier to swallow. The snake's skin stretches as the meal moves down its body.

6 As the vole moves further down inside the snake's body, the skin stretches more. The ribs move apart at the front to make space for the vole's body. The snake pushes its windpipe to the front of its mouth, so that it can use it like a snorkel for breathing. It may take only one or two gulps for a snake to swallow a small animal whole.

Venomous Snakes

Only about 700 species of snake are venomous. Snake poison, called venom, is useful for snakes because it allows them to kill without having to fight a long battle against their prey. Some snake venom works on the prey's body, softening it and making it easier to digest. There are two main kinds of venom. One type attacks the blood and muscles. The other attacks the nervous system, stopping the heart and lungs from working.

spitting cobra
(*Hemachatus haemachatus*)

▲ DEADLY BITE

A copperhead gets ready to strike. Venomous snakes use their sharp fangs to inject a lethal cocktail of chemicals into their prey. The death of victims often occurs in seconds or minutes, depending on the size of prey and where it was bitten.

▼ WARNING ENEMIES

The bright and bold stripes of coral snakes warn predators that they are extremely venomous. There are more than 50 species of coral snake, all with similar patterns. But predators remember the basic pattern and avoid all coral snakes.

▲ VENOM SPIT

Spitting cobras have an opening in their fangs to squirt venom into an enemy's face. They aim at the eyes, and the venom can cause blindness.

coral snake
(*Micruroides euryxanthus*)

Did you know? The most venomous snake in the world is the black-headed sea snake.

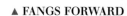

▲ **FANGS FORWARD**

The copperhead is a viper, so its fangs swing down from the roof of the mouth, ready to stab its prey. The muscles around the venom glands squeeze venom through the fangs.

copperhead
(*Agkistrodon contortrix*)

Bible Snake

At the beginning of the Bible, a snake is the cause of problems in the Garden of Eden. God told Adam and Eve never to eat fruit from the tree of knowledge of good and evil. However, the snake persuaded Eve to eat the fruit. It told Eve that the fruit would make her as clever as God. Eve gave some fruit to Adam too. As a punishment, Adam and Eve had to leave the Garden of Eden and lose the gift of eternal life.

▲ **MILKING VENOM**
Venom is collected from a black mamba.

green bush viper
(*Atheris squamigera*)

Focus on Vipers

Vipers are the most efficient venomous snakes of all. Their long fangs can inject venom deep into a victim. The venom acts mainly on the blood and muscles of the prey. Vipers usually have short, thick bodies and triangular heads covered with small, ridged scales. There are two main groups of vipers. Pit vipers have large heat pits on the face, and other vipers do not.

TREE VIPER
The green bush viper lives in tropical forests, mainly in the trees. Its green appearance means that it is well camouflaged against the green leaves. It lies in wait for its prey and then kills it with a quick bite. Once the prey has been caught, the snake must hold tight to stop it falling out of the tree.

BALLOON SNAKE
When threatened, the puff adder swells up like a long balloon. It does this by taking a lot of air into its lungs. Being larger makes it look even more dangerous. Puff adders also hiss loudly.

puff adder
(*Bitis arietans*)

34

rattlesnake
(*Crotalus*)

QUICK JAB

This rattlesnake is exploring its surroundings with its forked tongue. When the rattlesnake strikes at its prey, the hinged fangs swing forward and lock into place. The viper gives its prey a quick injection of venom, then lets go. The prey soon dies, so there is no need for the snake to hold on to it.

HEAT DETECTORS

This Sumatran pit viper has a large heat pit on each side of its head, between the nostril and the eye. The heat pit is larger than the nostril. It can detect the heat given off by warm-blooded prey. By turning its head from side to side, a pit viper can work out the direction of its prey.

Sumatran pit viper
(*Trimeresurus sumatranus*)

SLOW SNAKE

Asp vipers are slow-moving snakes. They are active both by day and by night. Their main sources of food are mice, lizards and baby birds.

35

Avoiding Enemies

The predators of snakes include birds of prey, foxes, racoons, mongooses, baboons, crocodiles, frogs and even other snakes. If they are in danger, snakes usually prefer to hide or escape. Many come out to hunt at night, when it is more difficult for predators to catch them. If they cannot escape, snakes often make themselves look big and fierce, hiss loudly or strike at their enemies. Some pretend to be dead. Giving off a horrible smell is another good way of getting rid of an enemy!

▶ **SMELLY SNAKE**
The cottonmouth is named after its mouth, which is white inside. If it is attacked, it opens its mouth to threaten enemies and it can also give off a strong-smelling liquid from near the tail.

◀ **EAGLE ENEMY**
The short-toed eagle uses its powerful toes to catch snakes. It eats large snakes on the ground. It carries small snakes back to the nest to feed its chicks.

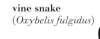
vine snake
(*Oxybelis fulgidus*)

◀ **SCARY MOUTH**
Like many snakes, this vine snake opens its mouth very wide to startle predators. The inside of the mouth is bright red and warns off the predator. If the predator does not go away, the snake will give a venomous bite with the fangs at the back of the mouth.

▶ PLAYING DEAD

This grass snake knows that most predators prefer healthy, living prey. So it protects itself by pretending to be dead. It rolls on to its back, opens its mouth and keeps quite still.

cottonmouth
(*Agkistrodon piscivorus*)

◀ DRAMATIC DISPLAY

The hognose snake is harmless, but can make itself look dangerous. It flattens its neck to make a hood. It hisses loudly and strikes towards the enemy. Then it smears itself with smelly scent.

▶ HIDDEN SNAKE

The horned viper buries itelf so that it cannot be seen by its enemies.

▲ LOOKING LARGER

The cobra spreads its hood wide to make itself look too big to swallow.

37

HOOD VARIETY

Like spitting cobras, the king cobra and the water cobra, this Egyptian cobra has a narrow hood. The Indian cobra and the Cape cobra of southern Africa have much wider hoods. The Egyptian cobra ranges over much of Africa and into Arabia.

HOOD PATTERNS

Some cobras have eyespots on the back of their hoods to make them look more scary.

THE HOOD

The cobra's hood is made from flaps of skin supported by long ribs. Mostly, the skin rests flat against the body. But when it is alarmed the cobra spreads its neck ribs, stretching the neck skin to form a hood.

Focus on the Cobra and its Relatives

Cobras are highly venomous snakes. Some of them can squirt deadly venom at their enemies. Cobra venom works mainly on the nervous system, causing breathing or heart problems. Cobras are members of the elapid snake family, which includes the African mambas, the coral snakes of the Americas and all the venomous snakes of Australia.

LARGE COBRA

The king cobra is the largest venomous snake, growing to a length of 5.5m (18ft). King cobras are the only snakes known to build a nest. The female guards her eggs and hatchlings until they leave the nest.

MIND THE MAMBA

The green mamba lives in trees. Other mambas, such as the black mamba, live mostly on the ground. Mambas are slim, long snakes that can grow up to 4m (13ft) long. Their venom is very powerful and can kill a person in only ten minutes!

DO NOT DISTURB!

The Australian mainland tiger snake is a member of the elapid snake family. It is the world's fourth most venomous snake. If it is disturbed, it puffs up its body, flattens its neck and hisses loudly. The diet of these snakes includes fish, frogs, birds and small mammals.

rainbow boa
(*Epicrates cenchria*)

◄ **CHANGING HUES**
The rainbow boa is iridescent. Light is made up of all the hues of the rainbow. When light hits the thin outer layer of the snake's scales, it splits into different shades. What we see depends on the type of scales and the way light bounces off them.

Patterns and Camouflage

Snakes get their patterns from the pigments in the scales and from the way light reflects off the scales. Dull shades help to camouflage a snake and hide it from its enemies. Brighter markings startle predators or warn them that a snake is venomous. Harmless snakes sometimes copy the markings of venomous snakes. Darker pigments may help snakes to absorb heat during cooler weather. Young snakes can look different from their parents, but no one knows why.

milk snake
(*Lampropeltis doliata*)

ring-necked snake
(*Diadophis punctatus*)

Did you know? Milk snakes always have black bands between the red and yellow – coral snakes have the red and yellow touching.

◄ **BRIGHT PATTERNS**
This snake's red tail draws attention away from the most vital part of its body – the head.

◀ COPYCAT

The bright red, yellow and black bands of this milk snake copy the appearance of the venomous coral snake. The milk snake is not venomous, but predators leave it alone – just in case! This is found in milk snakes in the southeast of the USA.

▼ ALBINO SNAKES

White snakes are called albinos. In the wild, these snakes stand out against the background and are usually killed by predators before they can reproduce.

▼ SNAKE MARKINGS

Many snakes are marked with striking patches. These markings are usually caused by groups of different pigments in the scales.

red-tailed boa
(*Boa constrictor*)

◀ CLEVER CAMOUFLAGE

Among the dead leaves of the rainforest floor, the gaboon viper becomes almost invisible. Many snakes have patterns that match their surroundings.

Reproduction

Snakes do not live as families, and parents do not look after their young. Males and females come together to mate, and pairs may stay together for the breeding season. Most snakes are ready to mate when they are between two and five years old. In cooler climates, snakes usually mate in spring so that their young have time to feed and grow before the winter starts. In tropical climates, snakes often mate before the rainy season, when there is plenty of food for their young. Male snakes find females by following their scent trails.

flowerpot snake
(*Typhlops braminus*)

▲ NO MATE
Scientists believe that female flowerpot snakes can produce young without males. This is useful when they move to new areas, as one snake can start a new colony. However, all the young are the same, and if conditions change, the snakes cannot adapt and may die out.

► FIGHTING
Male adders fight to test which one is the stronger. They rear up and face each other, then twist their necks together. Each snake tries to push the other to the ground. In the end, one of them gives up.

spur

◄ SNAKE SPURS
Both boa and python males have small spurs on their bodies. These are the remains of back legs that have disappeared as snakes have developed over millions of years. A male uses its spur to scratch or tickle the female during courtship, or to fight with other males. Females' spurs are usually smaller.

▲ WRESTLING MATCH

These male Indian rat snakes are fighting to see which is the stronger. The winner stands a better chance of mating. The snakes hiss and strike out, but they seldom get hurt.

► SIMILARITIES AND DIFFERENCES

No one knows why the male and female of the snake shown here have such different head shapes. In fact, male and female snakes of the same species usually look similar because snakes rely on scent rather than sight to find a mate.

male

Madagascar leaf-nosed snake
(*Langaha nasuta*)

female

◄ MATING

When a female anaconda is ready to mate, she lets the male coil his tail around hers. The male has to place his sperm inside the female's body to fertilize her eggs. The eggs can then develop into baby snakes.

Eggs

Some snakes lay eggs and some give birth to
fully developed, or live, young. Egg-laying
snakes include cobras and pythons. A few
weeks after mating, the female looks for a
safe, warm, moist place to lay between 6 and
40 eggs. This may be under a rotting log, in
sandy soil, under a rock or in a compost heap.
Most snakes cover their eggs and leave them
to hatch by themselves. A few snakes stay
with their eggs to protect them from
predators and the weather.
However, once the eggs hatch,
all snakes abandon their young.

▲ BEACH BIRTH
Sea kraits are the only sea snakes to
lay eggs. They often do this
in caves, above the
water level.

► EGG CARE
This female python has piled up her eggs
and coiled herself around them to protect
them from predators. The female Indian
python twitches her muscles to warm
up her body. The extra heat helps the
young to develop. Snake eggs need to be
kept at a certain temperature if they are
to develop properly.

◄ LAYING EGGS
The Oenpellis python lays rounded
eggs. The eggs of smaller snakes
are usually long and thin to fit
inside their smaller body.
Some snakes lay
long, thin eggs
when they are
young, but more
rounded eggs when
they grow larger.

Did you know? The mud snake lays over 100 eggs at a time.

▼ CHILDREN'S PYTHON MASS HATCHING

As they hatch, these children's pythons flatten their egg shells. A snake's egg shell is leathery, not brittle like the shell of a bird's egg. Birds' eggs would break into pieces if they were squashed. A snake's egg is not watertight, so it is laid in a moist place to stop it drying up.

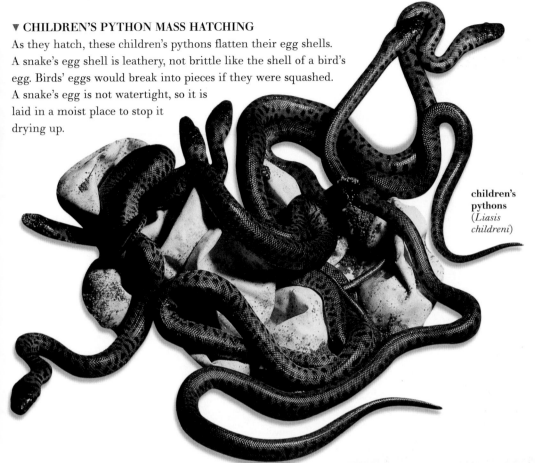

children's pythons (*Liasis childreni*)

▼ HIDDEN EGGS

Eggs are hidden from predators in the soil, or under rocks and logs. Eggs are never completely buried as the young need to breathe air that flows through the outer shell.

▲ HOT SPOTS

This female grass snake has laid her eggs in a warm pile of rotting plants.

45

Focus on Hatching Out

About two to four months after the adults mate, the baby snakes hatch out of their eggs. Inside the egg, the baby snake feeds on the yolk, which is full of goodness. Once the snake has fully developed and the yolk has been used up, the snake is ready to hatch. All the eggs in a clutch tend to hatch at the same time. A few days later, the baby snake wriggles away to start life without any parents.

1 Eight weeks after being laid, these rat snake eggs are hatching. While they developed inside the egg, each baby rat snake fed on its yolk. A day or so before hatching, the yolk sac was drawn inside the snake's body. A small scar, rather like a tummy button, will show where the snake was once joined to the yolk.

2 The baby snake has become restless, twisting inside its shell. It is now fully developed and cannot get enough oxygen through its shell. A snake's egg has an almost watertight shell, but water and gases, such as oxygen, pass in and out of it through tiny holes (pores). As the baby snake prepares to hatch, it cuts a slit in the shell with a sharp egg tooth on its snout. This egg tooth will drop off a few hours after hatching.

3 After it has broken through the stretchy shell, the baby snake has a rest. It pokes its nose through the slit in the egg to breathe the air and take a first look at the strange and exciting world outside.

4 All the eggs in this clutch have hatched at the same time (a clutch is a set of eggs laid by a snake). After making the first slits in their leathery shells, the baby snakes will not crawl out straight away. They poke their heads out of their eggs to taste the air with their forked tongues. If they are disturbed, they will slide back inside the shell where they feel safe. They may stay inside the shell for a few days.

Did you know? Some snakes lay as many as 100 eggs in one clutch.

5 Eventually, the baby snake slithers out of the egg. It may be as much as seven times longer than the egg because it was coiled up inside.

47

Pope's
tree viper
(*Trimeresurus
popeorum*)

Giving Birth

▲ TREE BIRTH

Tree snakes often give
birth in the branches. The
membrane around each baby snake
sticks to the leaves and helps stop the baby from
falling out of the branches to the ground.

Some snakes give birth
to fully developed or live young, instead
of laying eggs. Snakes that do this
include boas, rattlesnakes, adders and
most sea snakes. The eggs develop
inside the mother's body surrounded by
see-through bags, called membranes.
While the baby snake is developing
inside the mother, it gets its food from
the yolk of the egg. The babies are born
after a delivery that may last for hours.
Anything from 6 to 50 babies are born
at a time. At birth, they are still inside
their membranes.

▲ BIRTH PLACE

This female sand viper has chosen a quiet,
remote spot to give birth to her young. Snakes
usually give birth in a hidden place, where
the young are safe from enemies.

▶ BABY BAGS

These red-tailed boas have just
been born. They are still inside
their see-through bags. The bags
are made of a clear, thin, tough
membrane, rather like the one
inside the shell of
a hen's egg.

Did you know?
Newborn anacondas are only 6cm (2½in) long

► **BREAKING FREE**

This baby rainbow boa has just pushed its head through its surrounding membrane. Snakes have to break free of their baby bags on their own. Each baby has an egg tooth to cut a slit in the membrane and wriggle out. The babies usually do this a few seconds after birth.

Did you know? Baby boa constrictors are 30cm (12in) long when they are born.

◄ **NEW BABY**

A red-tailed boa has broken free of its baby bag, or egg sac, which is in the front of the picture. The baby's appearance is bright. Some newborn babies crawl off straight away, while others stay with their mother for a few days.

◄ **TURNING GREEN**

This vivid red baby is an emerald tree boa. As it grows up, it will turn green. Although boas and pythons are very similar snakes in some ways, one of the main differences between them is that boas give birth to live young while pythons lay eggs.

Did you know? Timber rattlesnake mothers defend their newborn babies for a few days.

emerald
tree boa
(*Epicrates
cenchria*)

Growth and Development

The size of baby snakes when they are born or when they hatch from their eggs, how much they eat and the climate around them all affect their rate of growth. In warm climates, snakes may double or triple their length in just one year. Some snakes are mature and almost fully grown after three to five years, but slow growth may continue throughout their lives. Young snakes shed their skin more often than adults because they are growing quickly. While they are growing, young snakes are easy prey for animals such as birds, racoons, toads and rats.

▼ FAST FOOD
Like all young snakes, this Burmese python must eat as much as possible in order to grow quickly. Young snakes eat smaller prey than their parents, such as ants, earthworms and flies.

▲ DEADLY BABY
This baby European adder can give a nasty bite soon after hatching. Luckily, its venom is not very strong.

mother
European
adder

baby
European
adder

▲ MOTHER AND BABY
European adders give birth in summer. The young must grow fast so that they are big enough to survive winter hibernation.

Burmese python
(*Python molurus
bivittatus*)

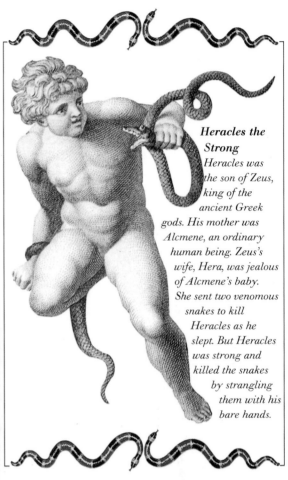

**Heracles the
Strong**
*Heracles was
the son of Zeus,
king of the
ancient Greek
gods. His mother was
Alcmene, an ordinary
human being. Zeus's
wife, Hera, was jealous
of Alcmene's baby.
She sent two venomous
snakes to kill
Heracles as he
slept. But Heracles
was strong and
killed the snakes
by strangling
them with his
bare hands.*

rattlesnake
(*Crotalus*)

short rattle

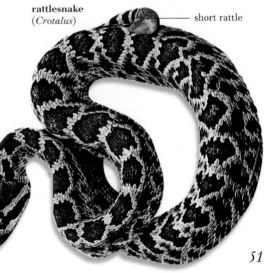

▲ DIET CHANGE
Many young Amazon tree boas live on islands in
the West Indies. They start off by feeding on
lizards, but as they grow they switch to feeding
on birds and mammals.

▶ RATTLE AGE
You cannot tell the age of a rattlesnake by
counting the sections of its rattle because
several sections may be added each year and
pieces of the rattle may break off.

51

Where Snakes Live

Snakes live on every continent except
Antarctica. They are most common in deserts
and rainforests. They cannot survive in very
cold places because they use the heat around
them to make their bodies work. This is why
most snakes live in warm places where the
temperature is high enough for them to stay
active day and night. In cooler places, snakes
may spend the cold winter months asleep.
This is called hibernation.

▲ **GRASSLANDS**
The European grass snake is one of the
few snakes to live on grasslands, where
there is little food or shelter.

◄ **MOUNTAINS**
The Pacific rattlesnake is
sometimes found in the mountains
of the western USA, often on the
lower slopes covered with
loose rock.
In general,
though,
mountains are
problem places for
snakes because of their
cold climates.

▲ **WINTER SLEEP**
Thousands of garter snakes emerge
after their winter sleep. Snakes often
hibernate in caves or underground,
where it is warmer.

▼ TROPICAL RAINFORESTS

The greatest variety of snakes lives in tropical rainforests, including this Brazilian rainbow boa. There is plenty to eat, from insects, birds and bats to frogs.

▲ LIVING IN TREES

The eyelash viper lives in the Central American rainforest. The climate in rainforests is warm all year round, so snakes can stay active all the time. There are also plenty of places to live – in trees, on the forest floor, in soil and in rivers.

Brazilian rainbow boa
(*Epicrates cenchria*)

► BURROWERS

Yellow-headed worm snakes live under tree bark. Many worm, or thread, snakes live under ground where the soil is warm.

◄ DESERTS

This African puff adder lives in the Kalahari desert of southern Africa. Many snakes live in deserts because they can survive with little food and water.

53

Tree Snakes

With their long, thin, flat bodies and pointed heads, tree snakes slide easily through the branches of tropical forests. Some can even glide from tree to tree. Tree boas and pythons have ridges on their belly scales to give them extra gripping power. Many tree snakes also have long, thin tails that coil tightly around branches. Green or brown camouflage patterns keep tree snakes well hidden among the leaves and branches.

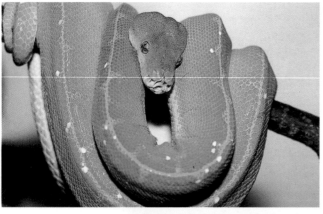

▲ **CAMOUFLAGE**
This Amazon tree boa has patterns for camouflage. Many tree snakes are green or brown with patterns that break up the outline of their body shape. Some even have patterns that look like mosses and lichens.

▲ **TREE TWINS**
The green tree python lives in the rainforests of New Guinea. It looks similar to the emerald tree boa and behaves in a similar way, but they are not closely related.

◀ **GRASPING**
In a rainforest in Costa Rica, a blunt-headed tree snake has caught a lizard. It grasps its prey firmly so that it does not fall out of the tree. Tree snakes have long, sharp teeth, good for piercing skin.

long-nosed whip snake
(*Ahaetulla mycterizens*)

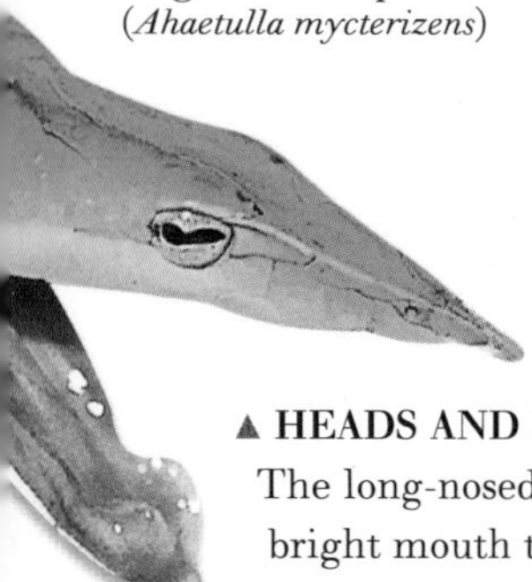

Did you know? Many snakes have long tails to grip tree trunks and branches.

▲ **HEADS AND EYES**

The long-nosed whip snake opens its
bright mouth to scare away a predator.
It has a long head, with a pointed snout — an
ideal shape for sliding through branches.

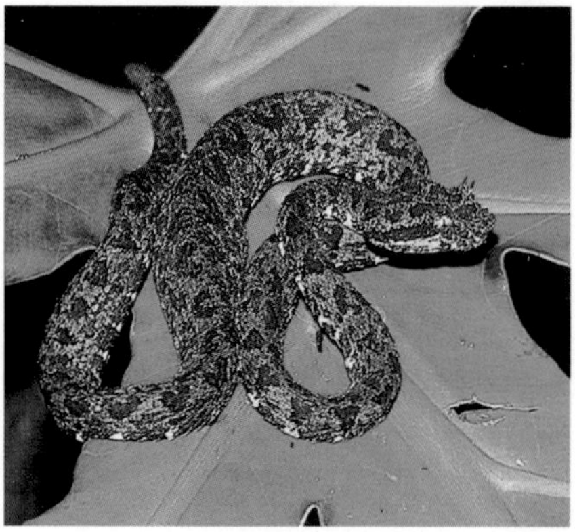

Cook's tree boa
(*Boa cookii*)

▲ **VIPER REFLEXES**

The green eyelash viper has such
speedy reflexes that it can catch birds
as they fly through the trees. It has to
hold on to its prey while its venom
takes effect.

▶ **BODY WEIGHT**

Tree snakes have long, thin,
light bodies. This helps them
to crawl along small branches
without breaking them. They can
also stretch easily from one branch
to another.

55

Focus on the Emerald

With their green coils looped around branches, emerald tree boas lurk among leaves in the rainforests of South America. These tree boas are good climbers, hanging head-first from branches to seize fast-moving prey in their teeth. To rest, they lie with their coils encircling a narrow branch, and their head lying on top.

UPSIDE-DOWN MEALS

To catch a meal, emerald tree boas drape their coils over a horizontal branch and hang their heads down. Once the snake has a firm hold on its prey with its teeth, it coils around its victim. It slowly squeezes with its coils to stop the animal breathing. When the animal is dead, the emerald tree boa swallows it head-first, so that it slides down easily.

CLIMBING SKILLS

Tree boas are longer and slimmer than boas that live on the ground. This helps them to slide through the branches.

GRIPPING

The emerald tree boa's tail grips the branch. As the boa climbs, it reaches up with its front end and coils itself around a branch, then pulls up the rest of its body.

Tree Boa

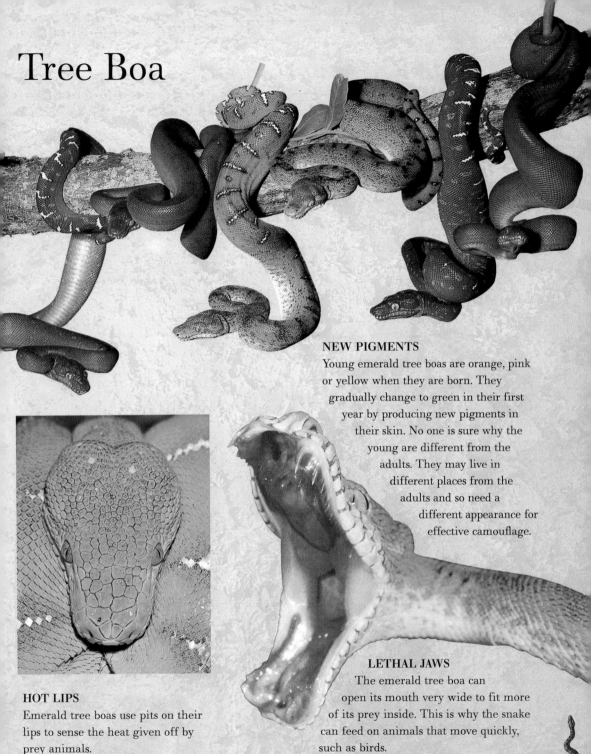

NEW PIGMENTS

Young emerald tree boas are orange, pink or yellow when they are born. They gradually change to green in their first year by producing new pigments in their skin. No one is sure why the young are different from the adults. They may live in different places from the adults and so need a different appearance for effective camouflage.

HOT LIPS

Emerald tree boas use pits on their lips to sense the heat given off by prey animals.

LETHAL JAWS

The emerald tree boa can open its mouth very wide to fit more of its prey inside. This is why the snake can feed on animals that move quickly, such as birds.

Desert Snakes

Deserts are full of snakes. This is partly
because snakes can survive for a long time
without food. They don't need to use energy
from food to produce body heat because they
get heat energy from their surroundings. It is
also because their waterproof skins stop them
losing too much water. Snakes push between
rocks or down rodent burrows to escape the
Sun's heat and the night's bitter cold. Some
snakes rest quietly underground during
very hot, dry periods.

◄ SCALE SOUNDS
If threatened, the desert
horned viper
makes a
loud
rasping
sound by
rubbing
together jagged
scales along the sides of its body. This
warns predators to keep away.

horned viper
(*Cerastes cerastes*)

► RATTLING
A rattlesnake
shakes its rattle to
warn enemies to
keep away. It
shakes its tail and
often lifts its head
off the ground. It
cannot hear the
buzzing noise it
makes – but its
enemies can.

▶ SAND SHUFFLE

The desert horned viper shuffles under the sand by rocking its body to and fro. It spreads its ribs to flatten its body and pushes its way down until it almost disappears. It strikes out at its prey from this position.

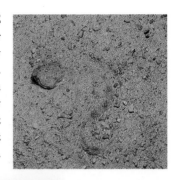

◀ SIDEWINDING

Many desert snakes, such as this Peringuey's viper, travel in a movement called sidewinding. As the snake moves, only a small part of its body touches the hot sand at any time. Sidewinding also helps to stop the snake sinking down into the loose sand.

◀ HIDDEN BOA

The patterns of this sand boa make it hard for predators and prey to spot among desert rocks and sand. The sand boa's long, round body shape helps it to burrow down into the sand.

The Hopi Indians

This Native North American was a Hopi snake chief. The Hopi people used snakes in their rain dances to carry prayers to the rain gods to make rain fall on their desert lands.

Water Snakes

Some snakes live in marshy areas or at the edge of freshwater lakes and rivers. Two groups of snakes live in salty sea water. They breathe air, but they can stay underwater for a long time. Glands on their heads get rid of some of the salt from the water. Sea snakes have hollow front fangs and are very venomous. This is because a sea snake has to subdue its prey quickly in order to avoid losing it in the depths of the sea.

◄ SEA SENSES

A sea snake's eyes and nostrils lie towards the top of the head. This means it can take a breath without lifting its head right out of the water, and the eyes can watch out for predators about to attack.

▼ CHAMPION SWIMMER
Northern water snakes are good swimmers, rarely found far from fresh water. They feed mainly on fish, frogs, salamanders and toads. At the first sign of danger, they dive under the water.

► BREATH CONTROL
Sea snakes have a large lung enabling them to stay underwater for a few hours.

◄ HEAVY WEIGHT

The green anaconda lurks in swamps and slow-moving rivers, waiting for birds, turtles and caimans to come within reach of its strong coils. Green anacondas weigh up to 227kg (500lb)!

sea krait
(*Laticauda colubrina*)

▲ LAND LUBBER

The sea krait is less well adapted to the water and lays eggs on land.

Snake Families

Scientists have divided the 2,700 different kinds of snake into about ten groups, called families. These are the colubrids, the elapids, the vipers, the boas and pythons, the sea snakes, the sunbeam snakes, the blind snakes and worm snakes, the thread snakes, the shieldtail snakes and the false coral snake. The snakes in each family have features in common. The biggest family is the colubrid family, with over 1,800 different species of snake.

Did you know?
The viper family includes rattlesnakes, adders, asps and pit vipers.

▲ COLUBRIDS
About three-quarters of all the world's snakes, including this milk snake, belong to the colubrid family. Most colubrids are not venomous. They have no left lung or hip bones.

▲ VIPERS
Snakes in this family, such as the sand viper, have long, hollow fangs that can be folded back inside the mouth when they are not needed.

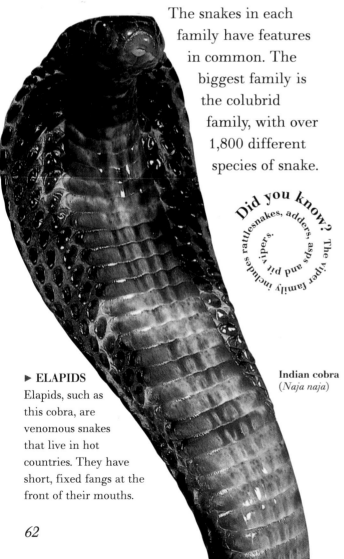

▶ ELAPIDS
Elapids, such as this cobra, are venomous snakes that live in hot countries. They have short, fixed fangs at the front of their mouths.

Indian cobra
(*Naja naja*)

Classification Chart		
	Kingdom ▼	Animalia ▼
	Phylum ▼	Chordata ▼
	Class ▼	Reptilia ▼
	Order ▼	Squamata ▼
	Suborder ▼	Ophidia ▼
	Family ▼	Boidae ▼
	Genus ▼	Boa ▼
	Species	Boa constrictor

This chart shows how a boa constrictor is classified within the animal kingdom.

Colombian
rainbow boa
(*Epicrates cenchria
maurus*)

► BOAS
AND
PYTHONS
This family
includes snakes that
kill by constriction rather than
poisoning. They have curved teeth,
hip bones and tiny back leg bones.

► SEA SNAKES
Some sea snakes are born in the sea
and spend all their lives there, and
others spend part of their time on land.
Sea snakes have flattened tails for
swimming and nostrils that can be
closed off under the water. Most live in
warm waters, from the Red Sea to New
Zealand and Japan.

◄ SUNBEAM SNAKES
The two members of the sunbeam family are burrowing
snakes that live in South-east Asia and southern China.
Unlike most other snakes, they have two working lungs,
though the left one is about half the size of the right.

63

sand lizard

Snake Relatives

Snakes are part of a large group of animals called reptiles. There are about 6,000 different kinds of reptiles, nearly half of which are snakes. Other reptiles include turtles and tortoises, lizards, crocodiles and alligators. Reptiles have bony skeletons with a backbone and bodies covered in scales. They lay eggs with waterproof shells or give birth to live young. Young reptiles look like copies of their parents. Reptiles are cold-blooded and rely on their surroundings for heat, so they live mostly in warm places.

▲ LIZARDS
This sand lizard is threatening an enemy by making itself look big and scary. Lizards have movable eyelids and good eyesight. Most lizards have pointed tongues.

Did you know? The largest reptile in the world is the saltwater crocodile, which grows over 7m (23ft) long.

baby crocodile

◄ CARING CROCODILES
Crocodiles are dangerous reptiles. Yet female crocodiles make doting mothers. They guard their eggs and protect their young until they can fend for themselves.

◄ LEGLESS LIZARDS

Some burrowing lizards have tiny legs – or none at all. Snakes possibly developed from burrowing lizards, which did not need legs for sliding through soil.

Did you know? The only two venomous lizards are the Gila monster and the Mexican bearded lizard.

▼ LIZARD TAILS

Lizards, like this water dragon, generally have long tails and shed their skin in several pieces.

water dragon

▼ TORTOISES

A tortoise has a shell as well as a skeleton. The shell is made from bony plates fused to the ribs, with an outer covering of horny plates. It is useful for protection, but it is also very heavy.

▼ BURROWING LIZARD

Worm lizards dig burrows underground with their strong, hard heads. Their nostrils close during burrowing so they do not get clogged up with soil.

tortoise

worm lizard

65

Conservation

Some snakes are killed because people are afraid of them. Farmers often kill snakes to protect their farm animals and workers, although many snakes actually help farmers by eating pests. In some countries snakes are killed for food or used to make medicines. To help snakes survive, people need to take action to preserve their habitats, so that snakes can live in safety.

▲ FINDING OUT MORE
Scientists use an antenna to pick up radio signals from a transmitter fitted to a rattlesnake. This allows them to track the snake even when they cannot see it. The more we can learn about snakes, the easier it is to protect them.

▲ TROPHY
There are still those who shoot snakes for recreation. The hunters put the snake's rattle or head on display as a trophy demonstrating their sporting achievements.

▶ SNAKES IN DANGER
Snakes, such as this Dumeril's boa, are in danger of dying out. Threats include people taking them from the wild and road building in places where they live.

▼ ROUND-UP

This show in North America demonstrates the skill of capturing a rattlesnake. Today rattlesnake hunts are not as common as they once were.

▲ USING SNAKE SKINS

Snake skins have been used for many years to make souvenirs. Some species have declined as a result of intensive killing for skins in some areas. Recently, countries such as Sri Lanka and India have banned the export of snake skins.

Did you know? Legend says St Patrick banished snakes from Ireland to rid the country of evil.

▼ PET SNAKES

Some people like to keep pet snakes. However, they can do very little and are not happy in captivity. Snakes can lose the ability to hunt and dislike being kept in a confined space.

CROCODILES

The biggest and most intelligent reptiles
are the crocodilians: crocodiles, alligators,
caimans and gharials, all of which hunt
and feed mainly in the water. The largest
crocodilians weigh as much as three cars
and are able to tackle prey as large as a
zebra or a even person. Most of them are
timid and lazy, though, spending their
days lurking in the water and waiting
for a meal to pass nearby. Unlike other
reptiles, crocodilians are social animals,
gathering in groups to bask in the sun,
share food, court and nest.

What is a Crocodilian?

Crocodilians are thick-skinned, scaly reptiles that include crocodiles, alligators, caimans and gharials. They are survivors from a prehistoric age – their relatives first lived on Earth with the dinosaurs nearly 200 million years ago. Today, they are the dinosaurs' closest living relatives, apart from birds.

Crocodilians are fierce predators. They lurk motionless in rivers, lakes and swamps, waiting to snap up prey with their enormous jaws and tough teeth. Their prey ranges from insects, frogs and fish to birds and large mammals, such as deer and zebras. Very few crocodilians regularly attack and kill humans. Most are timid. Crocodilians usually live in warm, tropical places in or near freshwater, and some live in the sea. They hunt and feed mainly in the water, but crawl on to dry land to sunbathe, nest and lay their eggs.

▲ SCALY TAILS
Like many crocodilians, an American alligator uses its long, strong tail to swim through the water. The tail moves from side to side to push the alligator along. The tail is the same length as the rest of the body.

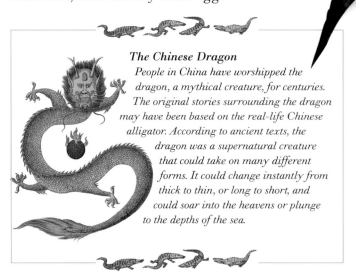

long, strong tail has flat sides to push aside water for swimming

The Chinese Dragon
People in China have worshipped the dragon, a mythical creature, for centuries. The original stories surrounding the dragon may have been based on the real-life Chinese alligator. According to ancient texts, the dragon was a supernatural creature that could take on many different forms. It could change instantly from thick to thin, or long to short, and could soar into the heavens or plunge to the depths of the sea.

► CROCODILIAN CHARACTERISTICS
With its thick, scaly skin, huge jaws and powerful tail, this American alligator looks like a living dinosaur. Its eyes and nostrils are on top of the head so that it can see and breathe when the rest of its body is underwater. On land, crocodilians slither along on their bellies, but they can lift themselves up on their four short legs to walk.

▲ TALKING HEADS

Huge, powerful jaws lined with sharp teeth make Nile crocodiles killing machines. They are some of the world's largest and most dangerous reptiles. The teeth are used to attack and grip prey, but are no good for chewing. Prey has to be swallowed whole or in chunks.

► SHUT EYE

Although this spectacled caiman has its eyes shut, it is probably not asleep, but dozing. Two butterflies are basking in safety on the caiman's head. Predators will not dare to attack them because the caiman is still aware of what is going on around it, even though its eyes are shut.

► SOAKING UP THE SUN

Nile crocodiles sun themselves on a sandbank. This is called basking and warms the body. Crocodilians are cold-blooded, which means that their body temperature is affected by their surroundings. They have no fur or feathers to keep them warm, nor can they shiver to warm up. They move in and out of the water to warm up or cool down.

the scales on the back are usually much more bony than those on the belly

scaly skin covers the whole body for protection and camouflage

Did you know? Most crocodilians live for about 50 years but some live up to 100.

eyes and nostrils on top of the head

digits (toes) of each foot are slightly webbed

American alligator (*Alligator mississippiensis*)

long snout with sharp teeth to catch prey

71

Croc or Gator?

There are 13 species (kinds) of crocodile; two species of alligator, six species of caimans; and two species of gharial. Gharials have distinctive long, slender snouts, but crocodiles and alligators are often more difficult to tell apart. Crocodiles usually have longer, more pointed snouts than alligators. Crocodiles also have one very large tooth sticking up from each side of the bottom jaw when they close their mouths.

▲ CAIMAN EYES
Most caimans have bonier ridges between their eyes than alligators. These ridges help strengthen the skull and look like the spectacles people wear to help them see. Caimans are usually smaller than alligators.

KEY
crocodiles
alligators/ caimans
gharials

▲ WHERE IN THE WORLD?
Crocodiles are the most widespread crocodilian and live in Central and South America, Africa, southern Asia and Australia. Caimans live in Central and South America, while alligators live in the south-eastern USA and China. The gharial is found in southern Asia, while the false gharial lives in South-east Asia.

▼ A CROCODILE'S SMILE
With its mouth closed, a crocodile's fourth tooth in the lower jaw fits into a notch on the outside of the upper jaw. No teeth can be seen on the bottom jaw of an alligator's closed mouth.

Chinese alligator
(*Alligator sinensis*)

▲ COOL ALLIGATOR
There are two species of alligator, the Chinese alligator (shown above) and the American alligator. Alligators are the only crocodilians that can survive cooler temperatures and live outside the tropics.

▶ DIFFERENT SNOUTS

Crocodilian snouts are different shapes and sizes because of the food they eat and the way they live. Gharials and crocodiles have narrow, pointy snouts suited to eating fish. Alligators, and caimans have wider, rounder snouts which can manage larger prey, such as birds and mammals. Their jaws are strong enough to overpower victims that are even larger than they are.

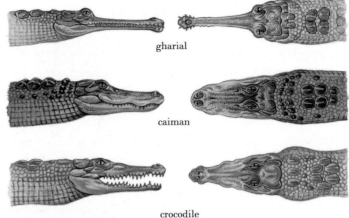

gharial

caiman

crocodile

◀ OUT TO SEA

The enormous saltwater crocodile, often called the saltie, has the largest range of all the crocodilians. It is found from the east coast of India through South-east Asia to the Philippines, New Guinea and northern Australia. Saltwater crocodiles are one of the few species found far out to sea, but they do live in freshwater rivers and lakes as well.

adult male gharials have a conspicuous knob at the tip of their snouts

▶ POT NOSE

Two species of gharial, the gharial, or gavial, and the false gharial, live in the rivers, lakes and swamps of southern Asia. The name comes from the knob on the nose of the male gharial, which is called a ghara (pot) in the Hindi language. Some experts say the false gharial is a species of crocodile and is therefore not really part of the gharial family.

gharial
(*Gavialis gangeticus*)

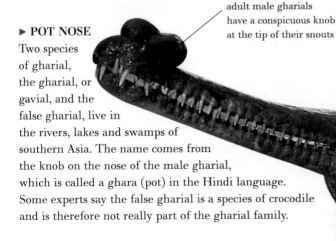

Large and Small

Can you imagine a crocodile that weighs as much as three cars? A big, 7m (23ft) long saltwater crocodile is as heavy as this. It is the heaviest living reptile in the world. Other enormous crocodilians include Nile crocodiles, gharials and American alligators, which can reach lengths of 5.5m (18ft) or more. Very large crocodiles and alligators are now rare because many are hunted and killed for their meat and skins before they grow to their maximum size. The smallest species of crocodilian are the dwarf caimans of South America and the African dwarf crocodile. These forest-dwelling reptiles grow to about 1.5m (5ft) long.

▲ BIGGEST CAIMAN
The black caiman is the largest of the caimans. It can grow to over 6m (19ft) long and is the biggest predator in South America. Black caimans live in the flooded Amazon forest, around lakes and slow-flowing rivers. They hunt at night for capybara, turtles, deer and fish.

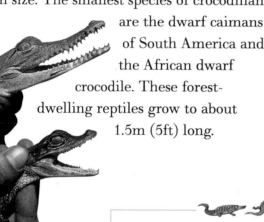

▲ A CROC IN THE HAND
A person holds a baby Orinoco crocodile (top) and a baby spectacled caiman (bottom). As adults, the Orinoco crocodile will be twice the length of the caiman, reaching about 5m (16ft). You can clearly see how the crocodile has a longer, thinner snout than the caiman.

Crocodile God
The ancient Egyptians worshiped the crocodile-headed god Sebek. He was the god of lakes and rivers, and is shown here with Pharaoh Amenhotep III. A shrine to Sebek was built at Shedet. Here, a Nile crocodile decorated with gold rings and bracelets lived in a special pool. It was believed to be the living god. Other crocodiles were also treated with great respect and hand-fed on meat, cakes, milk and honey.

◄ SUPER-SNOUTED CROCODILE

The mugger crocodile of India and surrounding lands has the broadest snout of all crocodiles, making it look more like an alligator. Adult males grow to about 4m (13ft). The name mugger comes from its habit of snatching fish out of people's fishing nets.

◄ SMALLEST CROCODILIAN

Cuvier's dwarf caiman is about a fifth of the size of a giant saltwater crocodile, yet it would still only just fit on your bed! It lives in the rainforests of the Amazon basin in South America. It has particularly tough skin to protect it from rocks in fast-flowing rivers. It has a short snout and high, smooth skull. Its short snout does not prevent it from eating a lot of fish.

Did you know? Male alligators keep growing until they are 15 years old

► MONSTER CROC

The huge Nile crocodile is the biggest and strongest freshwater predator in Africa. It can grow up to 6m (19ft) long and eats any prey it can overpower, including monkeys, antelopes, zebras and people. Nile crocodiles probably kill at least 300 people a year in Africa. Despite its name, the Nile crocodile is not just found along the Nile but also lives in rivers, lakes and swamps through most of tropical Africa.

A Scaly Skin

The outside of a crocodilian's body is completely covered in a thick hide. It is made up of rows of tough scales, called scutes, that are set into a thick layer of skin. Some scutes have small bony discs inside them. Most crocodilians have bony scutes only on their backs, but some, such as caimans, have them on their bellies as well. The tail never contains bony scutes, but it does have thicker tail scutes. As crocodilians grow, bigger scutes develop under the old ones. Crocodilians do not get rid of their old scaly skin in a big piece, like a snake, or in patches like a lizard. Old scutes drop off one at a time, just as humans lose flakes of skin all the time. On the head, the skin is fused directly to the bones of the skull without any muscles or fat in between.

Tricky Alligator
A Guyanese myth tells how the Sun was tricked by an alligator into letting him guard his fishponds from a thief. The thief was the alligator and to punish him the Sun slashed his body, forming the scales. The alligator promised the Sun his daughter for a wife. He had no children, so he carved her from a tree. The Sun and the woman's offspring were the Carob people.

▲ BABY PATTERNS
Most crocodilians have brightly patterned skin as babies, but these features usually fade as they grow older. They have more or less disappeared in the fully-grown adult. The patterns may help with camouflage by breaking up the outline of the body against its environment.

▲ THICK NECK
Heavy, bony scutes pack tightly together to create a rigid and formidable shield on the back and neck of an African dwarf crocodile. Even the scutes on the sides of its body and tail are heavily protected. This species lives in the dwindling rainforests of West and Central Africa. The small size and bony skin of the dwarf crocodile has saved it so far from being hunted for its skin.

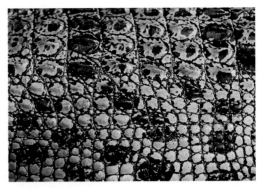

▲ MISSING SCALES

The gharial has fewer rows of protective scutes along its back than other crocodilians. Adults have four rows of deeply ridged back scutes, whereas other crocodilians have two or four extra rows in the middle of the back. The scutes on the sides and belly are unprotected.

▲ BONY BACK

The belly of a saltwater crocodile does not have bony plates in the scutes. You can see the difference in this close-up. Large, bony back scutes are shown at the top of the picture and the smaller, smoother belly scutes are at the bottom. The scutes are arranged in rows.

► EXTRA STRONG

This close-up shows the skin of a dwarf caiman – the most heavily protected crocodilian. It has strong bones in the scutes on its belly as well as its back. This provides protection from predators. Even its eyelids are protected by bony plates.

Did you know? The scales of the black caiman are as tough as the head of a tool.

► ALBINO ALLIGATOR

An albino (white) crocodilian would not survive long in the wild. It does not blend in well with its surroundings, making it easy prey. Those born in captivity in zoos or crocodile farms may survive to adulthood. True albinos are white with pink eyes. White crocodilians with blue eyes are not true albinos.

American alligator
(*Alligator mississippiensis*)

77

Bodies and Bones

The crocodilian body has changed very little over the last 200 million years. It is superbly adapted to life in the water. Crocodilians can breathe with just their nostrils above the surface. Underwater, ears and nostrils close and a transparent third eyelid sweeps across the eye for protection. Crocodilians are the only reptiles with ear flaps. Inside the long, lizard-like body a bony skeleton supports and protects the lungs, heart, stomach and other soft organs. The stomach is in two parts, one part for grinding food, the other for absorbing (taking in) nutrients. Unlike other reptiles, which have a single-chambered heart, a crocodilian's heart has four chambers, like a mammal. This allows the heart to pump more oxygen-rich blood to the brain during a dive. The thinking part of its brain is more developed than in other reptiles. This enables a crocodilian to learn things rather than act only on instinct.

▲ THROAT FLAP
A crocodilian has no lips so it is unable to seal its mouth underwater. Instead, two special flaps at the back of the throat stop water filling the mouth and flowing into the lungs. This enables the crocodile to open its mouth underwater to catch and eat prey without drowning.

Did you know? A saltwater crocodile can stay underwater for more than an hour.

◄ PREHISTORIC LOOKS
These American alligators look like their crocodilian ancestors that lived with the dinosaurs long ago. Crocodilians are the largest living reptiles. The heaviest is the saltwater crocodile which can reach up to 1,100kg (2,420lb).

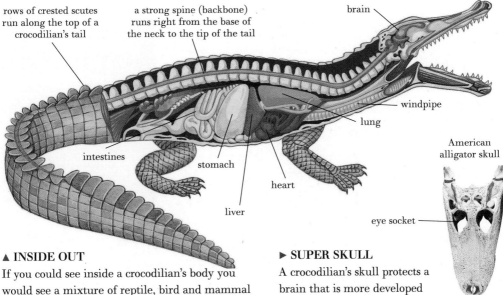

rows of crested scutes run along the top of a crocodilian's tail

a strong spine (backbone) runs right from the base of the neck to the tip of the tail

brain

windpipe

lung

intestines

stomach

heart

liver

American alligator skull

eye socket

American crocodile skull

▲ INSIDE OUT

If you could see inside a crocodilian's body you would see a mixture of reptile, bird and mammal features. The crocodilian's brain and shoulder blades are like a bird's. Its heart, diaphragm and efficient breathing system are similar to those of mammals. The stomach and digestive system are those of a reptile, as they deal with food that cannot be chewed.

▶ SUPER SKULL

A crocodilian's skull protects a brain that is more developed than any other reptile's. The skull is wider and more rounded in alligators (top), and long and triangular in crocodiles (bottom). Behind the eye sockets are two large holes where jaw muscles attach to the skull.

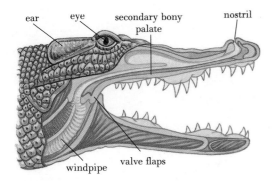

ear   eye   secondary bony palate   nostril

windpipe   valve flaps

▲ WELL DESIGNED

A view inside the head of a crocodilian shows the ear, eye and nostril openings set high up in the skull. The bones in the mouth are joined together to create a secondary bony palate that separates the nostrils from the mouth. Flaps of skin form a valve, sealing off the windpipe underwater.

▶ STOMACH STONES

Crocodilians swallow objects, such as pebbles, to help break down their food. These gastroliths (stomach stones) churn around inside part of the stomach, helping to cut up food so it can be digested. Some very unusual gastroliths have been found, such as bottles, coins, a whistle and a thermos flask.

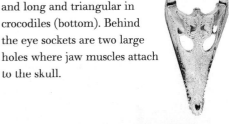

Jaws and Teeth

The mighty jaws of a crocodilian and its impressive rows of spiky teeth are lethal weapons for catching prey. Crocodilians have two or three times as many teeth as a human. The sharp, jagged teeth at the front of the mouth, called canines, are used to pierce and grip prey. The force of the jaws closing drives these teeth, like a row of knives, deep into a victim's flesh. The short, blunt molar teeth at the back of the mouth are used for crushing prey. Crocodilian teeth are no good for chewing food, and the jaws cannot be moved sideways to chew either. Food has to be swallowed whole, or torn into chunks. The teeth are constantly growing. If a tooth falls out, a new one grows through to replace it.

▲ MEGA JAWS
The jaws of a Nile crocodile close with tremendous force. They sink into their prey with tons of crushing pressure. Yet the muscles that open the jaws are weak. A thick elastic band over the snout can easily hold a crocodile's jaws shut.

◀ NEW TEETH FOR OLD
Each tooth is set in a socket and held in place by connective tissue. Throughout a crocodilian's life, the old teeth fall out and new teeth underneath take their place. Teeth last up to two years before falling out. Alternate teeth are replaced together, so that not all the teeth in one part of the mouth are lost at the same time.

◄ LOTS OF TEETH

The gharial has more teeth than any other crocodilian, around 110. Its teeth are also smaller than those of other crocodilians and are all the same size. The narrow, beak-like snout and long, thin teeth of the gharial are geared to grabbing fish with a sweeping sideways movement of the head. The sharp teeth interlock to trap and impale the slippery prey.

CHARMING

Crocodilian teeth are sometimes made into necklaces. People wear them as decoration or lucky charms. In South America, the Montana people of Peru believe they will be protected from poisoning by wearing a crocodile tooth.

▲ BABY TEETH

A baby American alligator is born with a full set of 80 teeth when it hatches from its egg. Baby teeth are not as sharp as adult teeth and are more fragile. They are like tiny needles. In young crocodiles, the teeth at the back of the mouth usually fall out first. In adults, it is the teeth at the front that are replaced more often.

► GRABBING TEETH

A Nile crocodile grasps a lump of prey ready for swallowing. If prey is too large to swallow whole, the crocodile grips the food firmly in its teeth and shakes its head hard so that any unwanted pieces are shaken off.

a Nile crocodile has 68 teeth lining its huge jaws

Did you know? A Nile crocodile may use 45 sets of teeth by the time it is 4m (12ft) long.

On the Move

Have you ever seen a film of an alligator gliding
through the water with slow, S-shaped sweeps of
its powerful tail? Crocodilians move gracefully
and easily in the water, using very little energy
and keeping most of their body hidden under the
surface. Legs lie close alongside bodies to make
them streamlined, and cut down drag from the
water. They may be used as rudders to change
course. On land, the short legs of crocodilians
make their walk look slow and clumsy, but they
can move quite fast if they need to. Some can
gallop at 18kph (11mph) when running for short
distances of up to 90m (295ft). Crocodilians also
move by means of the belly slide. With side-to-
side twists of the body, the animal uses its legs to
push along on its belly. This tobogganing
movement is useful for fast escapes, but is also
used to slip quietly into the water.

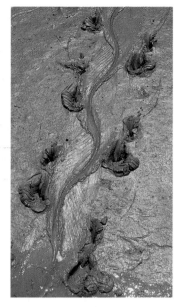

▲ BEST FOOT FORWARD
The tracks of a saltwater
crocodile in the mud show how
its legs move in sequence. The
right front leg goes forwards
first, then the back left leg.
The front left leg goes forward
next and finally the right back
leg. If the legs on the same side
moved one after the other, the
crocodile would overbalance.

▼ THE HIGH WALK
To move overland, crocodilians hold their legs underneath the
body, lifting most of the tail off the ground. This is called the
high walk. It is very different from the walk of a lizard, which
keeps its legs sprawled out at the sides of its body. The tail is
dragged behind the body in the high walk, but if the animal
starts to run, the tail swings from side to side.
A special ankle joint lets crocodilians
twist and turn their legs in the
stately high walk.

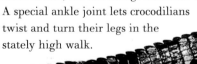

▲ FLOATING AROUND
This Nile crocodile is floating near the surface of Lake Tanganyika, Tanzania, Africa. It is holding its feet out to the sides for balance. The toes and the webbing between them are spread out for extra stability. In the water, the crocodile floats with its tail down, but as it moves its body becomes horizontal.

► TAIL WALKING
Some crocodilians leap straight up out of the water. They seem to be walking on their tails in the same way that a dolphin can travel backwards on its strong tail. This movement is unusual. Large crocodiles will also spring upwards, propelled by the back legs, to grab prey unawares.

► FEET AND TOES
On the front feet, crocodilians have five separate digits (toes). These sometimes have webbing (skin) stretched between them. The back feet are always webbed to help them balance and move in the water. There are only four toes on the back feet. The fifth toe is just a small bone inside the foot.

▲ THE GALLOP
The fastest way for a crocodilian to move on land is to gallop. Only a few crocodiles, such as the Johnston's crocodile shown above, make a habit of moving like this. In a gallop, the back legs push the crocodilian forward in a leap and the front legs stretch out to catch the body as it lands at the end of the leap. Then the back legs swing forward to push the animal forwards again.

Temperature Check

Soon after the sun rises, the first alligators heave themselves out of the river and flop down on the bank. The banks fill up quickly as more alligators join the first, warming their scaly bodies in the sun's rays. As the hours go by and the day becomes hotter, the alligators open their toothy jaws wide to cool down. Later in the day, they may go for a swim or crawl into the shade to cool off. As the air chills at night, the alligators slip back into the water again. This is because water stays warmer for longer at night than the land.

Crocodilians are cold-blooded, which means their body temperature varies with outside temperatures. To warm up or cool down, they move to warm or cool places. Their ideal body temperature is between 30–35°C (85–95°F).

▲ MUD PACK
A spectacled caiman is buried deep in the mud to keep cool during the hot, dry season. Mud is like water and does not get as hot or as cold as dry land. It also helps to keep the caiman's scaly skin free from parasites and biting insects.

◄ SOLAR PANELS
The crested scutes on the tail of a crocodilian are like the bony plates on dinosaurs. They act like solar panels, picking up heat when the animal basks in the sun. The scutes also move apart fractionally to let as much heat as possible escape from the body to cool it down.

◄ UNDER THE ICE

An alligator can survive under a layer of ice as long as it keeps a breathing hole open. Only alligators stay active at temperatures as low as 12–15°C (53–59°F). They do not eat, however, because the temperature is too low for their digestions to work.

▼ OPEN WIDE

While a Nile crocodile suns itself on a rock it also opens its mouth in a wide gape. Gaping helps to prevent the crocodile becoming too hot. The breeze flowing over the wide, wet surfaces of the mouth and tongue dries its moisture and, in turn, cools off its blood. If you lick your finger and blow on it softly, you will notice that it feels a lot cooler.

▲ ALLIGATOR DAYS

Alligators follow a distinct daily routine when the weather is good, moving in and out of the water at regular intervals. They also enter the water if they are disturbed. In winter, alligators retreat into dens and become rather sleepy because their blood cools and slows them down.

► MEAL BREAKS

Being cold blooded is quite useful in some ways. These alligators can bask in the sun without having to eat very much or very often. Warm-blooded animals such as mammals have to eat regularly. They need to eat about five times as much food as reptiles to keep their bodies warm.

Crocodilian Senses

The senses of sight, hearing, smell, taste and touch are much more powerful in a crocodilian than in other living reptiles. They have good eyesight and can identify different shades. Their eyes are also adapted to seeing well in the dark, which is useful because they hunt mainly at night. Crocodilians also have sharp hearing. They sense the sounds of danger or prey moving nearby and listen for the barks, coughs and roars of their own species at mating time. Crocodilians also have sensitive scales along the sides of their jaws, which help to feel and capture prey.

▲ NOISY GATORS
An American alligator bellows loudly during courtship. Noises such as hissing or snarling, are made at enemies. Young alligators call for help from adults. Small ear slits behind the eyes are kept open when the animal is out of the water. Flaps close to protect the ears when the animal submerges.

Did you know? Crocodiles shake their ear flaps up and down when they are angry.

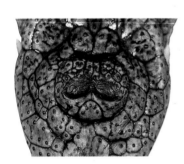

▲ SMELL DETECTORS
A Nile crocodile picks up chemical signals through the nostrils at the tip of its snout. These smelly messages help it to detect prey and others of its kind. Crocodiles can smell food over long distances. They are known to have come from as far away as 3km (2 miles) to feed on the carcass of a large animal.

Crocodile Tears
According to legend, crocodiles cry to make people feel so sorry for them that they come near enough for the crocodiles to catch them. Crocodiles are also supposed to shed tears of remorse before finishing their meal. It is said that people cry crocodile tears when they seem to be sorry for something, but really are not. Real-life crocodiles cannot cry but sometimes look as if they are.

▶ TASTY TONGUE

Inside the gaping mouth of an American crocodile is a wide, fleshy tongue. It is joined to the bottom of the mouth and does not move, so it plays no part in catching prey. We know that crocodilians have taste buds lining their mouths because some prefer one type of food to another. They can tell the difference between sweet and sour tastes. They also have salt glands on their tongues that get rid of excess salt. Salt builds up in the body over time if the animal lives in the sea or a very dry environment.

◀ GLOW-IN-THE-DARK EYES

A flashlight shone into a crocodile farm at night makes the dark glow eerily with a thousand living lights. The scientific explanation is that a special layer at the back of the eye reflects light back into the front of the eye. This makes sure that the eye catches as much light as possible. Above water, crocodilians see well and are able to spot prey up to 90m (295ft) away. Under water, an inner, transparent lid covers the eye. This makes their eyesight foggy, rather like looking through thick goggles.

▶ A PREDATOR'S EYE

The eye of a spectacled caiman, like all crocodilians, has both upper and lower lids. A third eyelid at the side, called a nictating (blinking) membrane, moves across to clean the eye's surface. The dark, vertical pupil narrows to a slit to stop bright light damaging the eye. At night, the pupil opens wide to let any available light into the eye. A round pupil, such as a human's, cannot open as wide.

Food and Hunting

How would it feel to wait up to two years for a meal? Amazingly, a big crocodile can probably survive this long between meals. It lives off fat stored in its tail and other parts of its body. Crocodilians eat a lot of fish, but their strong jaws will snap up anything that wanders too close, from birds, snakes and turtles to raccoons, zebras, cattle and horses. They also eat dead animals. Young crocodilians eat small animals such as insects, snails and frogs.

Most crocodilians sit and wait for their food to come to them, which saves energy. They also catch their meals by stealthily stalking and surprising prey. The three main ways of capturing and killing food are lunging towards prey, leaping up out of the water and sweeping open jaws from side to side through the water.

Most crocodilians hunt at night. They eat every part of their prey, including the bones.

▲ **SURPRISE ATTACK**
A Nile crocodile lunges from the water at an incredible speed to grab a wildebeest in its powerful jaws. It is difficult for the wildebeest to jump back as the river bank slopes steeply into the water. The crocodile will plunge back into the water, dragging its prey with it in order to drown it.

▼ **CHEEKY BIRDS**
Large crocodiles feed on big wading birds such as this saddlebill stork. Birds, however, often seem to know when they are in no danger from a crocodile. Plovers have been seen standing on the gums of crocodiles and even pecking at the fearsome teeth for leftovers. A marabou stork was once seen stealing a fish right out of a crocodile's mouth.

► SMALLER PREY

A dwarf caiman lies in wait to snap up a tasty bullfrog. Small species of crocodilian like this caiman, as well as young crocodilians, eat a lot of frogs and toads. Youngsters also snap up beetles, spiders, giant water bugs and small fishes. They will leap into the air to catch dragonflies and other insects hovering over the water. Small crocodilians are also preyed upon by their larger relatives.

crocodilians have varied diets and will eat any animal they can catch

◄ SWALLOWING PREY

A crocodile raises its head and grips a crab firmly at the back of its throat. After several jerky head movements the crab is correctly positioned to be eaten whole. High levels of acid in the crocodile's stomach help it break down the crab's hard shell so that every part is digested.

Did you know? A Nile crocodile has a stomach that is about the size of a basketball.

► FISHY FOOD

A Nile crocodile swallows a fish head first. This stops any spines it has sticking in the crocodile's throat. About 70 per cent of the diet of most crocodilians is fish. Crocodilians with narrow snouts, such as the gharial, Johnston's crocodile and the African slender-snouted crocodile, feed mainly on fish. Fish are caught with a sideways, snapping movement that is easier and faster with a slender snout.

Focus on a

1 A Nile crocodile is nearly invisible as it lies almost submerged in wait for its prey. Only its eyes, ears and nostrils are showing. It lurks in places where it knows prey regularly visit the river. Its dark olive skin provides effective camouflage. To disappear completely it can vanish beneath the water. Some crocodilians can hold their breath for more than an hour while submerged.

A crocodile quietly drifting near the shore looks just like a harmless, floating log. This is just a disguise as it waits for an unsuspecting animal to come down to the river to drink. The crocodile is in luck. A herd of zebras come to cross the river. The crocodile launches its attack with astonishing speed. Shooting forwards it snaps shut its powerful jaws and sharp teeth like a vice around a zebra's leg or muzzle. The stunned zebra is pulled into deeper water to be drowned. Other crocodiles are attracted to the large kill. They gather round to bite into the carcass, rotating in the water to twist off large chunks of flesh. Grazing animals constantly risk death-by-crocodile to drink or cross water. There is little they can do to defend themselves from the attack of such a large predator.

2 The crocodile erupts from the water, taking the zebras by surprise. It lunges at its victim with a quick burst of energy. It is important for the crocodile to overcome its prey quickly as it cannot chase it overland. The crocodile is also easily exhausted and takes a long time to recover from exercise of any kind.

Crocodile's Lunch

3 The crocodile seizes, pulls and shakes the zebra in its powerful jaws. Sometimes the victim's neck is broken in the attack and it dies quickly. More often the shocked animal is dragged into the water, struggling feebly against its attacker.

4 The crocodile drags the zebra into deeper water and holds it down to drown it. It may also spin round in a roll, until the prey stops breathing. The crocodile twists or rolls around over and over again, with the animal clamped in its jaws, until the prey is dead.

5 A freshly killed zebra attracts Nile crocodiles from all around. A large kill is too difficult for one crocodile to defend on its own. Several crocodiles take it in turns to share the feast and may help each other to tear the carcass apart. They fasten their jaws on to a leg or lump of muscle and twist in the water like a rotating shaft, until a chunk of meat is torn loose and can be swallowed.

Communication

Crocodilians pass on messages to each other by means of sounds, body language, smells and touch. Unlike other reptiles, they have a remarkable social life. Groups gather together for basking, sharing food, courting and nesting. Communication begins in the egg and continues throughout life. Adults are particularly sensitive to hatchling and juvenile distress calls and respond with threats or actual attacks. Sounds are made with the vocal cords and with other parts of the body, such as slapping the head against the surface of the water. Crocodilians also use visual communication. Body postures and special movements show which individuals are strong and dominant. Weaker individuals signal to show that they recognize a dominant individual and in this way avoid fighting and injury.

▲ **HEAD BANGER**
A crocodile lifts its head out of the water, jaws open. The jaws slam shut just before they smack the surface of the water. This is called the head slap and makes a loud pop followed by a splash. Head slapping may be a sign of dominance and is often used during the breeding season.

The Fox and the Crocodile
In this Aesop's fable, the fox and the crocodile met one day. The crocodile boasted at length about its cunning as a hunter. Then the fox said, "That's all very impressive, but tell me, what am I wearing on my feet?" The crocodile looked down and there, on the fox's feet, was a pair of shoes made from crocodile skin.

▲ **GHARIAL MESSAGES**
The gharial does not head slap, but claps its jaws under water during the breeding season. Sound travels faster through water than air, so sound signals are very useful for aquatic life.

▶ INFRASOUNDS

Some crocodilians make sounds by rapidly squeezing their torso muscles just beneath the surface of the water. The water bubbles up and bounces off the back. The sounds produced are at a very low level so we can hardly hear them. At close range, they sound like distant thunder. These infrasounds travel quickly over long distances through the water and may be part of courtship. Sometimes they are produced before bellowing, roaring or head slaps.

Did you know? The bellow of an alligator can be heard at least 150m (490ft) away.

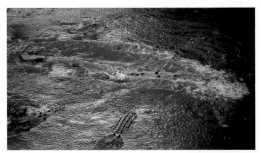

◀ I AM THE GREATEST

Dominant animals are usually bigger and more aggressive than submissive ones. They show off their importance by swimming boldly at the surface or thrashing their tails from side to side on land. Weaker individuals usually only lift their heads out of the water and expose their vulnerable throats. This shows that they submit and do not want to fight.

▶ GETTING TOGETHER

These caimans are gathering together at the start of the rainy season in Brazil. Crocodilians often come together in loose groups, for example when basking, nesting or sharing food. They tend to ignore each other once dominance battles have been established. During a long, dry spell, large numbers of crocodilians often gather together at water holes to share the remaining water. Young crocodilians stay in a close group for the first months of life as there is safety in numbers.

Choosing a Mate

Male and female crocodilians are often difficult to tell apart. Only male gharials are immediately recognizable, distinguished from females by the knob on the end of their snouts. Most males are larger, and grow and mature more quickly than females. They are ready to mate at about seven years old and females at about nine.

In some species, groups of adults gather together in the breeding season and set up special mating territories. In other species, mating takes place in long-established territories. Females often begin the courtship process. Courtship rituals can include bellowing and grunting, rubbing heads and bodies, blowing bubbles, circling and riding on the partner's back.

▲ POT NOSE
Most male gharials have a strange bump, or pot, on the end of the snout near the nostrils. Females have flat snouts. No-one is quite sure what the pot is for, but it is probably used in courtship. It may help the male to change hissing sounds into buzzing sounds as air vibrates inside the hollow pot.

◄ COURTING COUPLE
Crocodilians touch each other a lot during courtship, especially around the head and neck. Males will also try to impress females by bubbling water from the nostrils and mouth. An interested female arches her back, then raises her head with her mouth open. The two may push each other under the water to see how big and strong their partner is.

94

◄ **SWEET-SMELLING SCENT**
Crocodilians have little bumps under their lower jaws. These are musk glands. The musk is a sweet-smelling, greenish, oily perfume. It produces a scent that attracts the opposite sex. Musk glands are more noticeable in males. During courtship, the male may rub his throat across the female's head and neck. This releases the scent from the musk glands and helps to prepare the female for mating.

► **FIGHTING MALES**
Male crocodilians may fight each other for the chance to court and mate with females. They may spar with their jaws open or make themselves look bigger and more powerful by puffing up their bodies with air. Saltwater crocodiles are particularly violent and bash their heads together with a loud thud. These contests may go on for an hour or more but do not seem to cause much permanent damage.

◄ **THE MATING GAME**
Courtship can last for up to two hours before mating occurs. The couple sink under the water and the male wraps his tail around his partner. Mating takes only a few minutes. The couple mate several times during the day. A dominant male may mate with up to 20 females in the breeding season. Females, too, mate with other males, although the dominant male tries to prevent this.

Focus on

Early in April or May, American alligators begin courtship rituals. Males fight each other to win their own territories. The biggest and strongest males win the best territories. Their musk glands give off a strong, sweet smell, attractive to females. Female alligators do not have territories. They visit the territories of several males and may mate several times. Once a female and a male have mated, they part. The female builds a nest in June or July and lays her eggs. In about 60 to 70 days, the young alligators begin to hatch and the female digs them out of the nest and carries them to water. She remains with her young for months or even years.

1 Male and female alligators do not live together all year round. They come together in spring to court and mate. The rest of the year they glide through the swamp, searching for food or basking in the sun. In winter they rest in cosy dens.

2 The American alligator is the noisiest crocodilian. Males and females make bellowing noises especially in the breeding season. Males bellow loudly to warn other males to keep out of their territories and to let females know where they are. Each alligator has a different voice, which sounds like the throaty roar of a stalling motorboat engine. The sound carries for long distances in the swamp. Once one alligator starts to bellow, others soon join in and may carry on for half an hour.

Alligators

3 In the mating season bulls (males) test each other to see which is the biggest and strongest. They push and wrestle and sometimes fight violently. The strongest males win the best territories for food and water. Bellowing helps to limit serious fighting. Other males stay away from areas where they have heard a loud bull.

4 Alligators mate in shallow water. Before mating, there is a slow courtship made up of slapping the water and rubbing each other's muzzle and neck. Mating usually lasts only a minute or two before the pair separate. Alligators may mate with several partners in a season.

5 The female alligator uses her body, legs and tail to build a nest out of sand, soil and plants. It takes about two weeks to build and may be up to 75cm (30in) high and 2m (6ft) across. In the middle the female digs a hole and lines it with mud. She lays between 20 and 70 eggs, which she then covers up. She stays near the nest site while the eggs develop, guarding them from raccoons and other predators.

Building a Nest

About a month after mating, a female crocodilian is ready to lay her eggs on land. First she builds a nest to keep her eggs warm. If the temperature stays below 28°C (82°F), the babies will die before they hatch. The temperature inside the nest determines whether the hatchlings are male or female. Females build their nests at night. Alligators, caimans and some crocodiles build nests that are solid mounds of fresh plants and soil. Other crocodiles, and gharials, dig holes in the sand with their back feet. Some species dig trial nests before they dig the real one. This may be to check that the temperature is right for the eggs to develop. Nest sites are chosen to be near water but above the floodwater mark. The females often stay close to the nest to guard it against predators, even while searching for food.

▲ SHARING NESTS
Turtles, such as this red-bellied turtle, sometimes lay their eggs in crocodilian nests to save them the hard work of making their own nests. The eggs are protected by the fierce crocodilian mother, who guards her own eggs and the turtle's eggs. As many as 200 red-bellied turtle eggs have been found in alligator nests.

◄ NEST MOUNDS
A Morelet's crocodile has scratched soil and uprooted plant material into a big pile to build her nest mound. She uses her body to press it all together firmly. Then she scoops out a hole in the mound with her back feet. She lays her eggs in the hole and then closes the top of the nest. As the plant material rots, it gives off heat, which keeps the eggs warm.

Did you know? Male crocodilians do not help with making nests.

▼ IS IT A BOY OR A GIRL?

A saltwater crocodile, like all crocodilians, keeps its eggs at about 30–32°C (86–89°F) inside the nest. The temperatures during the first weeks after the eggs are laid is crucial – it controls whether the babies are male or female. Higher temperatures, such as 32–33°C (89–91°F) produce more males, while temperatures of 31°C (88°F) or lower produce more females. Temperature also affects the colour and body patterns of the babies.

▲ A SANDY NEST

Nile crocodiles dig their nests on sandy river banks, beaches or lakesides. Females may compete for nest sites by trying to push each other over. Larger, heavier females usually win these contests. The female uses her back legs for digging, so the nest burrow is dug to a depth of about the same length as her back legs.

► NESTING TOGETHER

Female Nile crocodiles often nest together. A female may even return to the same breeding ground and nest site each year. Each female guards her nest, either by lying right on top of the nest or watching it from the nearby shade.

◄ NEST THIEF

The monitor lizard often digs its way into crocodile nests in Africa and Asia to eat the eggs. In Africa, these lizards may sometimes steal over half of all the eggs laid.

Developing Eggs

All crocodilians lay white, oval eggs with hard shells like those of a bird. The number of eggs laid by one female at a time varies from about 10 to 90, depending on the species and the age of the mother. Older females lay more eggs. The length of time it takes for the eggs to hatch varies with the species and the temperature, but takes from 55 to 110 days. During this time, called the incubation period, the weather can affect the babies developing inside the eggs. Too much rain can drown the babies before they are born as water can seep through the shells. Hot weather may cause the inside of the egg to overheat. This hardens the yolk so that the baby cannot absorb it and starves to death. Another danger is that eggs laid by one female are accidentally dug up and destroyed by another female digging a nest in the same place.

▲ EGGY HANDFUL
In many countries, people eat crocodilian eggs. They harvest them from nests for sale at the local market. This person is holding the eggs of a gharial. Each egg weighs about 100g (3oz). The mother gharial lays about 40 eggs in a hole in the sand. She lays them in two tiers, separated from each other by a fairly thick layer of sand, and may spend several hours covering her nest.

▶ LAYING EGGS
The mugger, or swamp, crocodile of India digs a sandy pit about 50cm (20in) deep in a river bank and lays 10 to 50 eggs inside. She lays her eggs in layers and then covers them with a mound of twigs, leaves, soil and sand. During the 50- to 75-day incubation, the female spends most of the time practically on top of the nest. When females lay their eggs, they are usually quite tame. Researchers have been able to catch the eggs as they are laid.

► INSIDE AN EGG

Curled tightly inside its egg, this alligator has its head and tail twisted around its belly. Next to the developing baby is a supply of yolk, which provides it with food during incubation. Researchers have removed the top third of the shell to study the stages of development. The baby will develop normally even though some of the shell is missing. As the eggs develop, they give off carbon dioxide gas into the nest. This reacts with air in the chamber and may make the shell thinner to let in more oxygen.

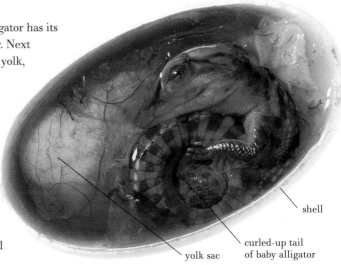

shell

curled-up tail of baby alligator

yolk sac

◄ CRACKING EGGS

Mother crocodiles sometimes help eggs to hatch. When she hears the baby calling inside, she picks up the egg in her mouth. Holding it gently, she rolls the egg to and fro against the roof of her mouth, pressing gently to crack the shell. The mother may have to do this for around 20 minutes before the baby breaks free from the egg.

Did you know? A large crocodile may take an hour to lay 80 or more eggs.

► EGGS IN THE NEST

Saltwater crocodiles lay large, creamy-white eggs, up to twice the size of chickens' eggs. However, the eggs are more equally rounded at each end than chicken's eggs. It takes a female saltwater crocodile about 15 minutes to lay between 20 and 90 eggs in her nest. The eggs take up to 90 days to hatch.

101

Focus on

Baby crocodilians make yelping, croaking and grunting noises from inside their eggs when it is time to hatch. The mother hears the noise and digs the eggs from the nest. The babies struggle free of their eggshells, sometimes with help from their mother. While the young are hatching, the mother is in a very aggressive mood and will attack any animal that comes near. The hatchlings are about 28cm (11in) long, lively and very agile. They can give a human finger a painful nip with their sharp teeth. Their mother carries them gently in her mouth down to the water. She opens her jaws and waggles her head from side to side to wash the babies out of her mouth.

1 As soon as a mother Nile crocodile hears her babies calling from inside their eggs, she knows it is time to help them escape from the nest. She scrapes away the soil and sand with her front feet and may even use her teeth to cut through any roots that have grown between the eggs. Her help is very important as the soil has hardened during incubation. The hatchlings would find it difficult to dig their way up to the surface without her help.

the hatchling punches a hole in its hard shell with a forward-pointing egg tooth

2 This baby Nile crocodile has just broken through its eggshell. It used a horny tip on the snout, called the egg tooth, to break through. The egg tooth is the size of a grain of sand and disappears after about a week. The egg has become thinner during the long incubation. This makes it easier for the baby to break free.

Hatching Out

3 Struggling out of an egg is a long, exhausting process for the hatchling. When the babies are half out of their eggs, they sometimes take a break so they can rest before completely leaving their shells. After hatching, the mother crushes or swallows rotten eggs.

4 Even though they are fierce predators crocodilians make caring parents. The mother Nile crocodile lowers her head into the nest and delicately picks up the hatchlings, as well as any unhatched eggs, between her sharp teeth. She gulps them into her mouth. The weight of all the babies and eggs pushes down on her tongue to form a pouch that holds up to 20 eggs and live young. Male mugger crocodiles also carry the young like this and help hatchlings to escape from their eggs.

5 A young crocodilian's belly looks fat when it hatches. This is because it contains the remains of the yolk sac, which nourished it through the incubation period. The hatchling can swim and catch its own food straight away, but it continues to feed on the yolk sac for up to two weeks. In Africa, the wet season usually starts soon after baby Nile crocodiles hatch. This provides an abundance of food, such as insects, tadpoles and frogs for the hatchlings. They are very vulnerable to predators and are guarded by their mother for at least the first weeks of life.

Growing Up

Juvenile (young) crocodilians lead a very dangerous life. They are too small to defend themselves easily, despite their sharp teeth. Their bright appearance also makes it easy for predators to spot them. All sorts of predators lurk in the water and on the shore, from birds of prey and monitor lizards to otters, pelicans, tiger fish and even other crocodilians. One of the reasons that crocodilians lay so many eggs is that so many young do not survive to reach their first birthday. Only one in ten alligators lives to the end of its first year. Juveniles often stay together in groups during the first weeks of life and call loudly to the adults for help if they are in danger. By the time the juveniles are four years old, they stop making distress calls and start responding to the calls of other young individuals.

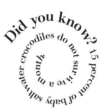

▲ INSECT DIET
A spiky-jawed Johnston's crocodile is about to snap up a damselfly. Juveniles eat mainly insects. As they grow, they take larger prey, such as snails, shrimps, crabs and small fish. Their snouts gradually strengthen, so that they are able to catch bigger prey. At a few months old, they live rather like lizards and move quite a distance away from the water.

Did you know? 15 percent of baby saltwater crocodiles do not survive a month.

◄ FAST FOOD
These juvenile alligators will grow twice as fast in captivity as they would in the wild. This is because they are fed regular meals and do not have to wait until they can catch a meal for themselves. It is also because they are kept in warm water — alligators stop feeding in cooler water. The best temperature for growth is 30–32°C (86–90°F).

▶ BABY CARRIERS

Juveniles stay close to their mother for the first few weeks, often using her back to rest on. No predator would dare to attack them there. Baby alligators are about 25cm (10in) long when they are born but they grow quickly. When they have enough food to eat, male alligators grow about 30cm (12in) a year until they are 15 years of age.

▲ CROC CRECHE

A Nile crocodile guards her young while they bask in the sun. A group of crocodilian young is called a pod. A pod may stay in the same area for as long as two years. At the first sign of danger, the mother rapidly vibrates her trunk muscles and the young immediately dive underwater.

▲ TOO MANY ENEMIES

The list of land predators that attack juvenile crocodilians include big cats such as this leopard, ground hornbills, marabou storks and genet cats. Large wading birds, including herons, spear them with their sharp beaks in shallow water, while, in deeper water, catfish, otters and turtles all enjoy a young crocodilian as a snack. Only about two per cent of all the eggs laid each year survive to hatch and grow into adults.

▶ NOISY POD

A pod of juveniles, like this group of young caimans, is a noisy bunch. By chirping and yelping for help, a juvenile warns its brothers and sisters that there is a predator nearby. The siblings quickly dive for shelter and hope that an adult will come to protect them. If a young Nile crocodile strays from its pod, it makes loud distress calls. Its mother, or any other female nearby, will pick up the youngster in her jaws and carry it back to the group.

On the Defensive

By the time a crocodilian has grown to about 1m (3ft) long, very few predators will threaten it. The main dangers to adult crocodilians come from large animals, such as jaguars, lions, elephants, and hippopotamuses, who attack to protect their young. Giant snakes called anacondas will attack and kill crocodilians for food. Adults may also be killed during battles with other crocodilians during the breeding season. People are the Number One enemy of crocodilians. They kill them for their skins, for food or because they are dangerous. Crocodilians are protected by their powerful jaws, strong tail and heavy, thick skin. They can also swim away from danger and hide under the water, in the mud or among plants.

▲ **KEEP AWAY!**
An American alligator puffs up its body with air to look bigger and more threatening. It lets out the air quickly to make a hissing sound. If an enemy is still not scared away, the alligator will then attack.

▶ **THE HIDDEN EYE**
What sort of animal is peeping out from underneath a green carpet of floating water plants? It is hard to tell that there is a saltwater crocodile lurking just beneath the surface. Crocodilians feel safer in the water because they are such good swimmers. They may spend hours almost completely under water, keeping very still, waiting for prey to come by or for danger to pass. They move so quietly and smoothly that the vegetation on top of the water is hardly disturbed.

▶ CAMOUFLAGE

Crocodilians blend in well with their surroundings. Many species change appearance all the time. For example, at warmer times of the day, they may become lighter. In cool parts of the day, such as the morning, they may look duller and are often mistaken for logs.

◀ CAIMAN FOR LUNCH

A deadly anaconda squeezes the life out of an unfortunate caiman. The anaconda of South America lives partly in the water and can grow up to 9m (30ft) long. It can easily kill a caiman by twisting its strong coils around the caiman's body until the victim cannot breathe any more. The caiman dies slowly, either from suffocation or shock. However, anacondas only kill caimans occasionally – they are not an important part of the snake's diet.

Ticking Croc
One of the most famous crocodiles in literature is in Peter Pan, *written by J. M. Barrie in 1904. Peter Pan's greatest enemy is Captain Hook. In a fair fight, Peter cut off Hook's left hand, which is eaten by a crocodile. The*

crocodile follows Hook's ship, hoping for a chance to gobble up the rest of him. It makes a ticking noise as it travels because it swallowed a clock. At the end, Hook falls into the water. He is chased by the crocodile, but we do not find out if he eats him.

▲ HUMAN DANGERS

People have always killed small numbers of crocodilians for food, as this Brazilian family have done. However, the shooting of crocodilians through fear or for sport has had a far more severe impact on their population. Of the 22 species of crocodilian, 17 have been hunted to the verge of extinction.

Freshwater Habitats

A habitat is a place where an animal lives. Most crocodilians live in freshwater (not salty) habitats, such as rivers, lakes, marshes and swamps, in warm places. They tend to live in the shallow areas on the edge of the water because they need to be able to crawl on to dry land for basking and laying their eggs. The shallow water also has many plants to hide among and plenty of animals to eat. The temperature of the water does not vary as much as temperatures on dry land do. This helps a crocodilian keep its body temperature steady. Crocodilians save energy by moving about in water rather than on dry land, because the water supports their heavy bodies. Crocodilians also make an impact on their habitats. The American alligator, for example, digs holes in the river bed. These are cool places where alligators and other animals hide during the heat of the day.

▲ GATOR HOLES
American alligators living in the Florida Everglades dig large gator holes in the limestone river bed. In the dry season, these holes stay full of water. They provide a vital water supply that keeps the alligators and many other animals alive.

Aboriginal Creation Myth
Crocodiles are often shown in bark paintings and rock art made by the Aboriginals of Australia. Their creation myth, called the dream time, tells how ancestral animals created the land and people. According to a Gunwinggu story from Arnhem Land, the Liverpool River was made by a crocodile ancestor. The mighty crocodile made his way from the mountains to the sea, chewing the land as he went. This made deep furrows, which filled with water to become the river.

▲ RIVER DWELLERS
The gharial likes fast-flowing rivers with high banks, clear water and deep pools where there are plenty of fish. It inhabits rivers such as the Indus in Pakistan, the Ganges in India and the Brahmaputra of Bangladesh and Assam.

◄ **SEASONAL CHANGE**
During the dry season, caimans gather in the few remaining pools along a drying-up river bed. Although the pools become very crowded, the caimans seem to get along well together. In some parts of South America, caimans are forced to live in river pools for four or five months of the year. After the floods of the wet season, they can spread out again.

► **NILE CROCODILES**

Nile crocodiles warm themselves in the sun on a sandy riverbank. Despite their name, Nile crocodiles do not live only in the river Nile. At one time, these powerful crocodiles lived all over Africa, except in the desert areas. Nowadays, they still live in parts of the Nile, as well as the other African waterways such as the Limpopo and Senegal rivers, Lake Chad and the Okavango swamp. There are also Nile crocodiles living on the island of Madagascar.

◄ **AUSTRALIAN HABITATS**
Australian crocodiles, such as Johnston's crocodile, often live in billabongs (waterholes) such as this one in the Northern Territory of Australia. They provide crocodiles with water and land as well as food to eat. A billabong is a branch of a river that comes to a dead end. Saltwater crocodiles are also found in such areas because they live in both fresh and salt water. People are advised not to swim or wade in the water and to avoid camping nearby.

Rainforest Dwellers

Three unusual crocodilians live in rainforest streams and swamps where they avoid competition with larger caimans and crocodiles. Cuvier's dwarf caiman and Schneider's dwarf caiman live in South America, while the African dwarf crocodile lives in the tropical forests of Central Africa. The bodies of these small crocodilians are heavily protected. This may help to protect the South American caimans from sharp rocks in the fast-flowing streams where they live and from spiky plants in the forest. All three crocodilians may also need this extra protection from predators because of their small size. Rainforest crocodilians do not usually bask in the sun during the day, although the dwarf crocodile may sometimes climb trees to sun itself. All three crocodilians seem to spend quite a lot of time on land. Schneider's dwarf caiman lives in burrows dug in stream banks.

▲ **MYSTERY CROC**

Very little is known about the African dwarf crocodile. It is a secretive and shy animal that is active at night. It lives in swamps, ponds and small, slow-moving streams. After heavy rain, the dwarf crocodile may make long trips over land at night. Females lay about ten eggs, which take 100 days to hatch. They probably protect their young in their first weeks.

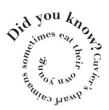

Did you know? Cuvier's dwarf caimans sometimes eat their own young.

◄ **YOUNG CAIMANS**

A newly hatched Cuvier's dwarf caiman rests on a rock. Hatchling dwarf caimans have a yellowish-brown skull and black or brown cross bands on the body and tail. This gives good camouflage. For the first couple of days, they are also covered in slime. Then they enter the water for the first time.

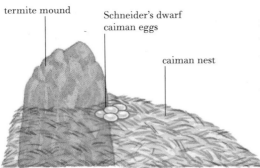

termite mound

Schneider's dwarf caiman eggs

caiman nest

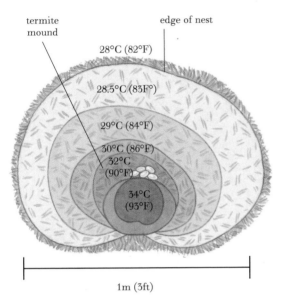

termite mound

edge of nest

28°C (82°F)

28.5°C (83F°)

29°C (84°F)

30°C (86°F)

32°C (90°F)

34°C (93°F)

1m (3ft)

◄ HELPFUL TERMITES

Schneider's dwarf caiman lays its eggs beside termite mounds. Little sun reaches the forest floor, so the extra heat generated by the termites helps the caiman's eggs develop. Often, the termites cover the eggs with a rock-hard layer, so the parents must help their young break out.

▲ NOSE TO TAIL

Unlike other caimans, dwarf caimans do not have bony ridges around the eyes and snout. Because of this they are also known as smooth-fronted caimans. Shown here is Cuvier's dwarf caiman. Its short snout is not streamlined for swimming and it has a short tail, which may help it to move more easily on land.

◄ TEETH AND DIET

The sharp, pointed teeth of Cuvier's dwarf caiman curve backwards in the mouth. This helps it grip the slippery skin of frogs or seize such prey as fish in fast-flowing waters. The Cuvier's diet is not well known, but it probably eats a variety of aquatic invertebrates (animals without a backbone), such as shrimps and crabs, as well as rodents, birds and snakes.

MARKINGS FOR LIFE
A black caiman hatches from its egg.
Its mother laid up to 65 eggs in the
nest, which hatched six weeks later.
Its strong markings stay as it grows.

THE SPECTACLED CAIMAN
The spectacled caiman is so-called
because of the bony ridges around its
eye sockets and across the top of the
muzzle. These look a bit like eye
glasses and may help to strengthen its
skull as it seizes and kills prey.

BIG HEAD
The broad-snouted caiman has the
widest head of any crocodilian, with a
ridge running down the snout. It is
about 2m (6ft) long and lives in marshes
or small streams with dense vegetation.

Focus on

Caimans are small, agile crocodilians that
live in Central or South America. Most do
not grow more than 2.4m (7ft) long, but the
black caiman can be bigger than an alligator
(their closest relative). Caimans look like
alligators because their lower teeth do not
show when their mouths are closed. They
have sharper, longer teeth than alligators and
strong, bony plates on the belly and back,
including eight bony scutes on the back of
the neck. This bony skin helps to protect
them from predators, even humans (as tough
skin is unsuitable for leather goods). Many
caimans are endangered, but some spectacled
caimans are very adaptable. They have taken
over habitats where American crocodiles and
black caimans have been hunted to extinction.

Caimans

MEMBERS OF THE GATOR CLAN

Caimans have short snouts, roughly circular eye sockets and wrinkled eyelids. Although caimans are closely related to alligators, they are quicker and move more like crocodiles.

young caimans and alligators have spots and bands across the body

black caiman
(*Melanosuchus niger*)

bony scutes

unusual webbed front feet

short, low snout with jaws lined with 64 teeth

EGG THIEF

Tegu lizards eat caiman eggs. In some areas, over 80 per cent of the nests are destroyed by these large lizards. Female caimans may nest together to help defend their eggs.

CAPABLE CAIMAN

The black caiman is the largest of all caimans. The one shown here has just snapped up a piranha fish. Black caimans can grow to over 6m (19ft) long and have keen eyesight and hearing. They hunt for capybaras (South American rodents) and fish after dusk. When black caimans disappear, the balance of life in an area is upset. Hunted for killing cattle, they are now an endangered species.

Saltwater Species

Most crocodilians live in fresh water, but a few venture into estuaries (the mouths of rivers), coastal swamps or the sea. American and Nile crocodiles and spectacled caimans have been found in saltwater habitats. The crocodilian most often seen at sea is the saltwater crocodile, also known as the Indopacific or estuarine crocodile. It is found over a vast area, from southern India to Fiji in the Pacific Ocean, and although usually found in rivers and lakes, it has been seen hundreds of miles from the nearest land. "Saltie" hatchlings are even reared in seawater. This species has efficient salt glands on its tongue to get rid of extra salt without losing too much water. It is a mystery why freshwater crocodiles also have these glands, but it may be because their ancestors lived in the sea. Alligators and caimans do not have salt glands.

▲ SALTY TONGUE
Crocodiles have up to 40 salt glands on the tongue. These special salivary glands allow the crocodile to get rid of excess salt without losing too much water. These glands are necessary because crocodiles have kidneys that need plenty of fresh water to flush out the salt. At sea there is too little fresh water for this to happen.

▶ SCALY DRIFTER
Although it can swim vast distances far out to sea, a saltwater crocodile is generally a lazy creature. Slow, side-to-side sweeps of a long, muscular tail propel the crocodile through the water, using as little energy as possible. Saltwater crocodiles do not like to have to swim vigorously, so they avoid strong waves wherever possible. They prefer to drift with the tide in relatively calm water.

▶ NEW WORLD CROC

The American crocodile is the most widespread crocodile in the Americas, ranging from southern Florida, USA, to the Pacific coat of Peru. It grows up to 6m (19ft) in length – 3.4m (11ft) on average – and lives in mangrove swamps, estuaries and lagoons as well as fresh and brackish (slightly salty) coastal rivers. It has the least bony scutes of any crocodilian and a hump on the snout between the eyes and nostrils.

◀ BABY CAIMANS

A group of baby spectacled, or common, caimans hides among the leaves of aquatic plants. This wide-ranging species lives in all sorts of habitats, including saltwater ones, such as salt marshes. They even live on islands, such as Trinidad and Tobago in the Caribbean.

◀ LESS PROTECTION

A saltwater crocodile has less protective skin on the neck and back compared to other crocodilians. This makes it easier for the crocodile to bend its body when swimming. Thick, heavy scales would weigh it down too much at sea.

▲ NILE CROCODILE

Nile crocodiles typically live in rivers, but they also inhabit salty estuaries and mangrove swamps. Sometimes they are found on Kenyan beaches and may be swept out to sea. Some have reached the islands of Zanzibar and Madagascar.

115

Ancient Crocodiles

The first alligators and crocodiles lived at the same time as the dinosaurs. Some were even powerful enough to kill the biggest plant-eating dinosaurs. Unlike the dinosaurs, the crocodilians have managed to survive to the present day, possibly because they were so well adapted to their environment. The first crocodiles, the protosuchians, lived about 200 million years ago. They were small land animals with long legs and short snouts. From 200 to 66 million years ago, long-snouted mesosuchians lived mainly in the sea, while the dinosaurs dominated the land. The closest ancestors of today's crocodilians were the early eusuchians, which developed about 80 million years ago. They looked rather like gharials, with long snouts, and probably lurked in the shallow fresh water of rivers and swamps. Like today's crocodilians, the eusuchians could breathe through their nostrils even when their mouths were open underwater. This made it possible for them to catch their prey in the water.

▲ FIRST CROCODILE

The name of this ancient crocodile, *Protosuchus*, means first crocodile. It lived about 200 million years ago in Arizona and looked rather like a lizard. *Protosuchus* was small, probably no more than 1m (3ft) long, with a small, flat skull and a short snout.

▼ BACK TO THE SEA

Swimming along the shores and estuaries in Jurassic times, from about 200 to 145 million years ago, the most widespread crocodilian was *Stenosaurus*. It looked rather like modern-day gharials, although it is not related to them. *Stenosaurus* had a flexible body and a powerful tail, which allowed it to swim after fast-moving prey.

long, slender snout and up to 200 piercing teeth for trapping fish

▶ DINOSAUR DAYS

Goniopholis, shown here, was more dependent on land than many of its fellow mesosuchians. It looked rather like a broad-snouted crocodile of today. *Goniopholis* had two or more rows of toughened skin on its back and thick skin on its belly as well. Most mesosuchians lived in the sea. They were long-snouted with many piercing teeth for catching fish.

◀ MONSTER CROCODILE

Lurking in the rivers and lakes of 70 million years ago was a gigantic crocodile called *Deinosuchus*, which grew perhaps 15m (50ft) long. It was a similar size to *T. rex* and big enough to eat quite large dinosaurs, such as the duck-billed dinosaurs. It had strong teeth and legs, vertebrae (spine bones) that were each 30cm (12in) long and heavy protective scales shielding the body and the tail.

▶ SURVIVORS

Crocodilians are survivors of a world inhabited by dinosaurs. However, the origins of both dinosaurs and crocodilians date back much further, to a group of animals called thecodontians, which lived some 200 million years ago.

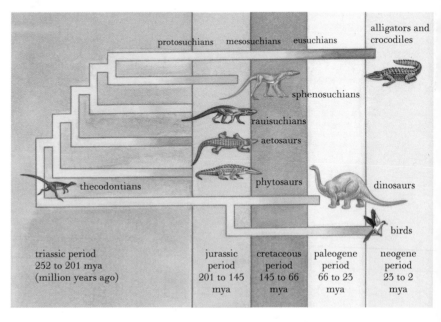

protosuchians   mesosuchians   eusuchians   alligators and crocodiles

sphenosuchians

rauisuchians

aetosaurs

thecodontians   phytosaurs   dinosaurs

birds

triassic period
252 to 201 mya
(million years ago)

jurassic period
201 to 145 mya

cretaceous period
145 to 66 mya

paleogene period
66 to 23 mya

neogene period
23 to 2 mya

117

Crocodile Relatives

Although it seems strange, birds are probably the closest living relatives of crocodilians. Crocodilians and birds have a long outer ear canal, a muscular gizzard to grind up food and a heart made up of four chambers. They both build nests and look after their young. The next closest living relatives of crocodilians are the group of reptiles called lepidosaurs, which includes the tuatara of New Zealand, lizards and snakes. The skin of lepidosaurs is usually covered by overlapping scales made of keratin (the substance fingernails are made of). Crocodilians and lepidosaurs both have two large openings on the cheek region of the skull, called a diapsid skull. Crocodilians are also more distantly related to the other main group of reptiles, turtles and tortoises.

▲ NESTING HABITS
The nests of some birds, such as this mallee fowl, are very similar to those of crocodilians. The mallee fowl builds a huge mound of wet leaves and twigs covered with wet sand. The female then lays her eggs in the middle of the mound.

▼ DINOSAUR SURVIVOR
The rare tuatara is found only on a few islands off the north coast of New Zealand. Here there are no rats or dogs to eat their eggs and hatchlings. They have hardly changed in appearance for millions of years and first appeared before dinosaurs lived on Earth.

▲ A SANDY NEST
Green turtles live in the sea, but lay their eggs on sandy beaches. The female drags herself up the beach and digs a hole in which to lay her eggs. Then she returns to the sea, leaving the baby turtles to fend for themselves when they eventually hatch.

▶ DIAPSID SKULLS

Crocodilians, and lizards such as iguanas, both have two large openings on each side of the skull behind the eye sockets. One of these windows is high on the roof of the skull, the other is down on the side of the cheek. These openings may be to make the skull lighter. They also provide areas for the jaw muscles to join on to the skull, making it stronger and more powerful. In birds, the two openings have largely disappeared. Mammals have only one opening on each side not two, while turtles have no openings at all.

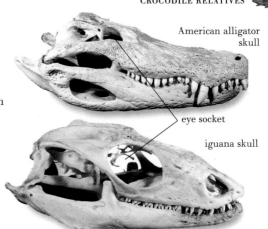

American alligator skull

eye socket

iguana skull

red-tailed boa

▲ REPTILE PREDATOR

Snakes are also scaly, meat-eating reptiles, but they catch prey in very different ways from a crocodilian. They have delicate bodies and need to overpower prey quickly before it can inflict an injury. Some, such as this boa, squeeze their prey to death in their powerful coils. Others kill their prey with a venomous bite.

Did you know? The sex of baby turtles is also controlled by temperature.

▶ MONSTROUS LIZARD

The gila monster of North America is a lizard with small, bead-like scales. It is one of the world's two poisonous lizards and its bright markings are a warning sign of its poisonous nature. The poison is produced in glands in the bottom jaw and chewed into both predators and prey. Crocodilians have much larger scales than lizards, and none are poisonous.

Living with People

Many people only ever see a crocodile or an alligator in a story book, on the television or at the cinema. These crocodilians are often huge, fierce monsters that attack and eat humans. Such images have given crocodilians a bad name. A few large crocodiles, such as Nile and saltwater species, can be very dangerous, but most are timid creatures that are no threat to humans. Some people even keep baby crocodilians as pets. Humans are a much bigger threat to crocodilians than they are to us. People hunt them for their skins to make handbags, shoes and belts. Traditional oriental medicines are made from many of their body parts. Their bones are ground up to add to fertilizers and animal feed. Their meat and eggs are cooked and eaten, while perfume is made from their sex organs, musk and urine.

▲ **ALLIGATOR DANGER**
The just-seen head of an American alligator reinforces why swimming is not allowed. Alligators lurking under the water do occasionally attack people. This usually only happens when humans have invaded its habitat or disturbed its nests or hatchlings.

▶ **CROCODILE DUNDEE**
One of the most dangerous and aggressive crocodilians is the saltwater crocodile, which appeared in the film *Crocodile Dundee*. In the film, Mick "Crocodile" Dundee, saves an American journalist from a surprise attack by a saltie. An adult saltie can grow up to 7m (23ft) long and is likely to view a human entering its territory as a possible meal.

Krindlekrax

In Philip Ridley's 1991 story, Krindlekrax, *a baby crocodile from a zoo escapes into a sewer and grows enormous on a diet of discarded toast. It becomes the mysterious monster Krindlekrax, which lurks beneath the pavements of Lizard Street. It is eventually tamed by the hero of the book, weedy Ruskin Splinter, who wedges a medal down the crododile's throat. He agrees to take the medal away if Krindlekrax will go back to the sewer and never come back to Lizard Street again.*

▲ SKINS FOR SALE

These saltwater crocodile skins are being processed for tanning. Tanning converts the hard, horny, preserved skin into soft, flexible leather that can be made into bags, wallets, shoes and other goods. Some of the most valuable skins come from saltwater crocodiles, because they have small scales that have few bony plates inside.

a false, glass eye has been inserted into the head

▲ ALLIGATOR WALKABOUT

An American alligator walks through a campsite, giving the campers a close-up view. Attacks out of the water are unlikely – the element of surprise is lost and alligators cannot move fast. Meetings like this are harmless.

▶ TOURIST SOUVENIRS

A baby Siamese crocodile was killed so that its head could be made into a key ring as a tourist souvenir. Most tourists never manage to see a wild crocodilian, but if they buy souvenirs such as this, it means more animals will be killed for a cruel trade.

Rare Crocodilians

Almost half of all of crocodilian species are endangered, even though there is much less hunting today than in the past. Until the 1970s, five to ten million crocodilians were being killed each year — far too many for them to reproduce and build up their numbers again. Today, the loss of habitat is a greater threat than hunting for most crocodiles. Other problems include illegal hunting, trapping for food and medicine, and the harvesting of crocodile eggs. Many species are not properly protected in national parks and there are not enough crocodilians being reared on farms and ranches to make sure each species does not disappear for ever. The four most endangered species are the Chinese alligator, the Philippine, Siamese and the Orinoco crocodiles. Other species that only live in small populations are the Cuban crocodile, black caiman and the gharial.

▲ HABITAT DESTRUCTION
The trees beside this billabong in Australia have died because there is too much salt in the water. Farmers removed many of the bush plants, which used to trap salt and stop it sinking down into the ground. Now much of the land is ruined by high levels of salt and it is difficult for crocodilians and other wildlife to live there.

▶ FISHING COMPETITION
People fishing for sport as well as for food create competition for crocodilians in some areas. They may also accidentally trap crocodilians underwater in their fishing nets so that they cannot come up for air, and drown. In waterways that are used for recreation, such as angling, bathing and boating, crocodilians may be killed by the blades of a motorboat's engine and because they pose a threat to human life.

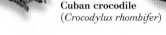

◄ CUBAN CROCODILE
This crocodile has the smallest range of any living crocodilian and is seriously endangered. It lives only on the island of Cuba and the nearby Isle of Pines. The growth of charcoal burning has drastically reduced the habitat of the Cuban crocodile. It has also moved into coastal areas and rivers, where it is more in danger from hunters.

Cuban crocodile
(*Crocodylus rhombifer*)

► SIAMESE CROCODILE
This endangered crocodile has almost died out in the wild. It was once found over large areas of South-east Asia, but wild Siamese crocodiles now live only in Thailand. They have become so rare because of extensive hunting and habitat destruction. They now survive mainly on crocodile farms.

▲ ILLEGAL HUNTING
This poacher has speared a caiman in the Brazilian rainforest. Hunting crocodilians is banned in many countries, but people still hunt illegally in order to make money. Their hides are so valuable that, even though this caiman's skin contains many bony scutes, it is still worthwhile taking the soft parts.

▼ UNWANTED CROCODILE
A small saltwater crocodile that strayed into somebody's garden is captured so it can be returned to the wild. Its jaws are bound together with rope to stop it biting the ranger. One of the biggest problems for crocodilians is the fact that more and more people want to live in the same places that they do.

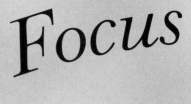
Focus

The gharial of northern India and the false gharial of South-east Asia are both endangered species. Their numbers have fallen due to hunting for their skins, habitat loss and competition for their main food, fish. Many of the fast-flowing rivers in which they live have been dammed to provide water for crops and to generate electricity. Dams flood some areas and reduce the flow of water in others, as well as damaging the river banks where gharials nest. People collect their eggs for food and believe them to have medicinal properties. To save the gharial, young are reared in captivity and released into the wild. The false gharial, however, does not breed well in captivity.

WELL ADAPTED
Gharials have a paler and slender body with extensive webbing between the toes on the back feet. Their long back legs are relatively weak. Gharials are well adapted for life in the water but are not fast swimmers.

CAPTIVE SURVIVAL
This gharial was bred in captivity and has been released into the wild. It has a radio tag on its tail so that scientists can follow its movements. In the 1970s, there were only about 300 wild gharials left. Captive breeding has increased numbers to over 1,500.

MEAL TIME
A gharial lunges sideways to snap up a meal from a passing shoal of fish. Predatory catfish are a popular meal. When gharial numbers went down, more catfish survived to eat the tilapia fish that local villagers caught for food.

on Gharials

FALSE IDENTITY
The false gharial looks like the true gharial and is probably related to it. It lives farther south than the true gharial, from southern Thailand to Borneo and Sumatra. In the wild, adults do not seem to help young escape from the nest and many die as they fend for themselves after hatching. Habitat loss and an increase in land used for rice farming have made false gharials rare. In Indonesia, over-collection of juveniles for rearing on farms may also have reduced numbers.

SAFE HOUSE
A scientist collects gharial eggs so that they can be protected in a sanctuary. There no predators will be able to get at them and the temperature can be kept just right for development. In the wild, about 40 per cent of eggs are destroyed by predators. Only about 1 per cent of the young survive to adulthood.

WATER SPORT
In the dry, low-water months of winter, gharials spend a lot of time basking on sand banks. Even so they are the most aquatic crocodilian. They move awkwardly when leaving the water and do not seem able to do the high walk like other crocodilians. Female gharials do not carry their young to the water. This is probably because their snouts are too slender and delicate and their teeth too sharp.

Conservation

Although people are frightened of crocodilians, they are a vital part of the web of life in tropical lands. They dig water holes that help other animals survive in dry seasons and clean up the environment by eating dead animals. Scientists find them interesting because they are good at fighting disease and rarely develop cancers. They are also fascinating to everyone as survivors from a prehistoric lost world. We need to find out more about their lives in the wild so we can help them to survive in the future. Some species, such as the American alligator, the saltwater crocodile and Johnston's crocodile of Australia and the gharial have already been helped by conservation measures. Much more work needs to be done, however, such as preserving their habitats, stopping illegal poaching and smuggling, breeding rare species in captivity and releasing them into the wild.

▲ CROCODILE FARMS
Tourists watch a wrestler show off his skill at a crocodile farm. The farm breeds crocodiles for their skins, attracting tourists as extra income. Farms help stop crocodiles being taken from the wild. The Samutprakan Crocodile Farm in Thailand has helped to save the rare Siamese crocodile from dying out by breeding them in captivity.

► RESEARCH REFUGE
Research at the Rockefeller Wildlife Refuge in Louisiana, USA, helped to work out the best way of rearing American alligators in captivity. They are brought up in special hothouses where temperature, humidity, diet, space and disease can be controlled. They have piped music so they will be less disturbed by outside noises. In these conditions, the alligators grow more than 1m (3ft) a year – much faster than in the wild.

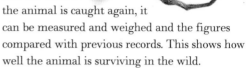

The tag on the foot of a black caiman helps identify it once it has been released into the wild. If the animal is caught again, it can be measured and weighed and the figures compared with previous records. This shows how well the animal is surviving in the wild.

▲ INTO THE FUTURE

This boy from Guyana is holding a baby dwarf caiman. Small numbers of caimans are sold as exotic pets. If people are paid more money for a living specimen than a dead one, they are less likely to kill crocodiles for skins. Educating people about why crocodilians are important is an important way of ensuring their future.

▶ RANCHING AND FARMING

A Nile crocodile is fed at a breeding station in South Africa. Crocodilians grow well on ranches or farms where they are fed properly. These places also provide information about the biology, health and feeding patterns of the reptiles.

◀ A NEW HOME

A row of black caimans, saved from a ranching scheme in Bolivia, wait to be flown to the Beni Biosphere Reserve, where they will be protected. The number of black caimans has dropped dramatically, and the animals they used to eat have increased as a result. This has caused problems for people, such as capybaras eating crops and piranhas attacking cattle.

127

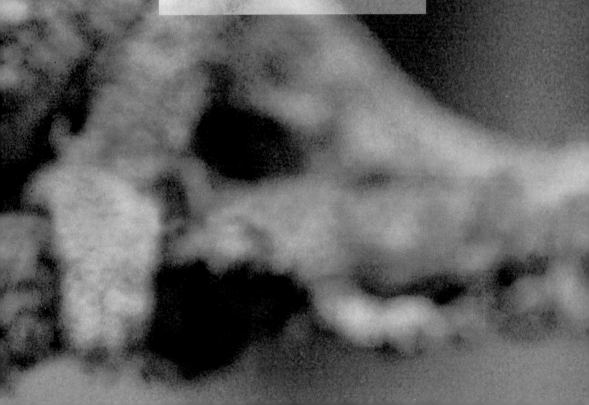

LIZARDS

The largest and most widespread group of
reptiles, lizards come in a great variety
of shapes and sizes, from giant Komodo
dragons and tiny geckos to camouflaged
chameleons and slow-worms with no legs
at all. Lizards live nearly everywhere on
land, even in baking deserts and on cold
mountains. The only true ocean-going
lizard is the marine iguana of the
Galapagos Islands. Most lizards are small
and vulnerable to predators, but their large
numbers, fast movement, spines and other
body coverings help to protect them.

Top Reptiles

Lizards form the largest group of reptiles, with almost 4,000 different species known. They are found in more places than any other type of reptile, living everywhere from deserts to the Arctic tundra, and exposed mountain slopes to isolated islands. A lizard's habitat can be anything from the highest branches in a forest's trees to the soil beneath its leaf-litter. Like all living reptiles, lizards are cold-blooded, which means that their body temperature varies with that of their surroundings. Most are small and feed on insects, but some have become large, dangerous carnivores. A few eat only plants. Lizards are very varied in appearance. The majority have four legs but some have lost their legs entirely and look like snakes.

▲ FIVE TOES, FOUR LEGS
This green lizard is a typical lizard. It is active by day and has four legs, each with five toes. Most lizards are fairly small; in the food chain they sit between insects and the predatory birds, mammals and snakes.

▼ LIZARD EGGS
Reptiles lay their eggs on land. Their eggs are cleidoic, which means 'closed-box' – the baby develops inside the egg, isolated from the outside world and often protected by a tough, leathery shell. Nutrition is supplied by the yolk sac, and waste products are stored in a membrane called the allantois. The amnion, a protective, fluid-filled membrane, surrounds the growing baby lizard and the yolk sac.

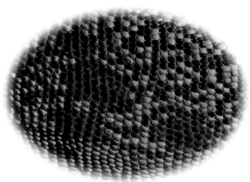

▲ SCALY SKIN
Lizards are covered in scales made of a substance called keratin, which is also the basis of human hair. Lizard scales vary in size from the tiny grain-like scales on geckos to the large, fingernail-like scales, or scutes, of plated lizards. Scales offer protection against injury and drying out.

MEGA MONITORS ▶

Lizards first appeared 100–150 million years ago. *Megalania priscus* was a giant Australian monitor lizard that would have made a Komodo dragon, the world's largest living lizard, look quite puny. Adults grew to 7m (23ft) and may have weighed more than half a ton. They probably ate prehistoric kangaroos and giant wombats. *Megalania* lived until 25,000 years ago and may have met Australia's first humans.

7m (23ft)

2m (6ft)

Megalania priscus

3m (10ft)

man

Komodo dragon

◀ GIANT DRAGONS

The heaviest lizard in the world is the Komodo dragon from the group of islands of the same name in Indonesia. Although there are stories of 5m (6½ft)-long Komodo dragons, the longest specimen ever accurately measured was 3.1m (10ft). It can weigh up to 70kg (155lb). The Salvador's monitor lizard from New Guinea, a more slimline and lighter relative, may grow longer, to over 4m (13ft).

MINI MARVELS ▶

The Nosy Be pigmy chameleon from northern Madagascar grows to no more than 3.4cm (1½in) long, but it is not the smallest living lizard. Even smaller is the Jaragua gecko from the Dominican Republic in the Caribbean. It grows to a maximum length of just 1.6cm (½in) and was discovered in 2001. Not only is it the world's smallest lizard, it is also the smallest land-living vertebrate (animal with a backbone) known to science.

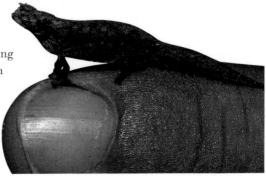

Lizard Relatives

The first reptiles appeared on Earth over 260 million years ago. Most types that lived in the distant past, such as dinosaurs and flying pterodactyls, are extinct today. Even so the Class Reptilia currently contains over 7,000 living species, ranging from turtles to crocodiles and geckos to snakes. All reptiles have scaly or leathery protective skin, which allows them to survive in salty, hot or dry conditions that would kill many other animals. Most lay leathery-shelled eggs, but a few lizards and snakes bear live young – an adaptation to living in colder climates where eggs would die. This versatility makes reptiles excellent survivors. Even though we now live in the Age of Mammals, reptiles are still a very successful group.

▲ RELATION WITH A SHELL

Turtles and tortoises belong to an ancient order of reptiles that split from the main reptile line shortly after the ancestors of mammals did. They are distantly related to other modern reptiles – in fact, lizards are related less to turtles and tortoises than they are to dinosaurs or birds. Turtles live in the sea and fresh water, while tortoises live on land.

▲ DINOSAUR DINNER

In this reconstruction, a plant-eating *Iguanodon* is being stalked by two meat-eating *Deinonychus*. Although dinosaurs might look like giant lizards they were more closely related to crocodiles and birds. Unlike modern reptiles, many dinosaurs walked on two legs. Most of these ancient reptiles were plant-eaters but some ate meat.

▲ FIERCE HUNTER

Crocodiles and alligators include the largest reptiles alive today. Nile crocodiles such as this can grow to 6m (20ft) long and weigh almost a ton, and the Indo-Pacific crocodile is even larger. Crocodilians eat meat and spend most of their time in water. They are distantly related to lizards and, like all egg-laying reptiles, they lay eggs on land.

Congo Monster

People living in the Congo rainforest claim it is inhabited by a giant Diplodocus-*like creature that they call Mokele-mbembe. Do dinosaurs still walk the Earth or could the monster be a large monitor lizard standing on its hind feet and stretching out its long neck? Several expeditions have set out in search of Mokele-mbembe but the mystery remains unsolved.*

THE FAMILY TREE ▼

As this tree shows, reptiles are a very diverse group. Turtles split away from the main reptilian line millions of years ago. Reptiles then divided into two main groups. The Archosauria (ancient reptiles) became dinosaurs, crocodilians and birds. The Lepidosauria (scaled reptiles) includes tuataras, and modern lizards, snakes and amphisbaenians (worm-lizards).

▲ TWO TUATARAS

These reptiles live on islands off the coast of New Zealand. Although they look like lizards, they have their own reptile group. They have hardly changed their appearance and habits since dinosaurs walked the Earth. Only two species of tuatara are alive in the world today.

▼ LEGLESS LIZARDS

Amphisbaenians, or worm-lizards, are legless reptiles that evolved from lizards. There are around 130 species, living in Florida, north-western Mexico, the West Indies, South America, Africa and Mediterranean Europe. Burrowers in soil and sand, amphisbaenians feed on earthworms and other invertebrates.

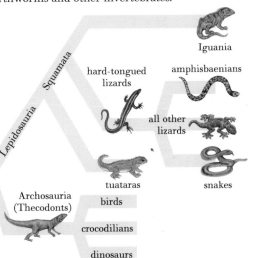

133

The Iguania

Lizards are split into two main groups. The first of these is known to scientists as the Iguania, and contains over 1,300 species, including iguanas, agamas, chameleons, anoles, swift lizards, lava lizards, basilisks and spiny lizards. The Iguania is an ancient group of reptiles dating back almost 100 million years. It is split into two smaller groups because agamas and chameleons have different teeth and live on different continents to iguanas and most of their relatives. Although some agamas look like iguanas, this is because they have become alike as a result of having similar lifestyles, and not because they are closely related.

▲ AMAZING AGAMAS

There are around 300 species of agama, living in south-eastern Europe, Asia, Africa and Australia. Many agamas are sun lovers, and include desert-dwellers such as the frilled lizards and this eastern bearded dragon. This family also contains the tiny flying lizards of South-east Asia and the secretive rainforest dragons of New Guinea and Queensland in Australia.

CHANGING CHAMELEONS ▶

This veiled chameleon comes from the Yemen, on the Arabian Peninsula. With their 'turret-eyes', curly prehensile tails, famous changing capabilities and long, sticky tongues, the chameleons must be the strangest family of lizards in the world. Although most of the 160 species live in Africa or Madagascar, the Indian chameleon comes from southern Asia and the European chameleon is found in southern Spain and Crete.

Did you know? Chameleons can change the appearance of their skin to match their surroundings.

IGUANAS AND CHUCKWALLAS ▶
Most iguanas, and their close relatives the chuckwallas, live in the Americas. Many are found in the West Indies, including the powerful rhinoceros iguanas. The Central and South American green iguana is perhaps the most familiar lizard in the world, but not all iguanas are American. The iguana on the right is from Fiji, in the Pacific Ocean.

SWIFT SPECIES ▶
This Cuvier's Malagasy swift lives in the dry scrub and rocky outcrops of Madagascar, a large island off the eastern coast of Africa. In all, seven insect-eating species of small, tree- and rock-dwelling swifts live there. They lay four to six eggs. Another family of small fast-moving lizards known as swifts come from the Americas, from the USA down to Argentina.

▲ **NATIVE KNIGHTS**
The knight anole is a native of Cuba, but it was introduced to southern Florida in 1952. There it hunts down the smaller green anole, which has become an endangered species in Florida, although it lives in many other parts of the world, including Hawaii. There are about 400 species of anoles in South America and the West Indies.

DASHING BASILISKS ▶
The plumed basilisk is the largest species of basilisk. The four species, together with the helmeted and cone-headed lizards, make up a small rainforest-dwelling family from Central America and northern South America. They are sometimes called 'Jesus lizards' because they can dash across water for some distance before breaking the surface.

OUT OF AFRICA
Jackson's three-horned chameleon inhabits woodland on the slopes of Africa's Mount Kenya, but may also be found in the suburbs of Kenya's capital city Nairobi. Males have longer horns than females. Small populations have become established on the Hawaiian Islands after pet Jackson's chameleons were released.

GIANT OF THE FORESTS
Parson's chameleon can reach 68cm (27in) long. This giant from Madagascar is the second-largest chameleon, after Oustalet's chameleon, which also comes from Madagascar. Parson's chameleon is an inhabitant of the island's wet eastern forest, and rarely changes appearance.

Focus on

When most people think of a chameleon they imagine a lizard with horns that can change its appearance to blend in with the surroundings. This 'typical chameleon' image does not do justice to this diverse family of lizards. Most of the 160 or so species are split fifty-fifty between Africa and Madagascar, but there is also a species in southern Europe, one on the Arabian peninsula and another in India. Not all chameleons live in rainforests – many inhabit dry woodland and some are found in deserts. The idea of chameleons being green lizards that can change appearance is also a generalization – some of the smaller species are brown and they cannot change at all.

EASTERN EGGS
The South-east Asian chameleon or Indian chameleon is found from Pakistan through India to northern Sri Lanka. The only truly Asian chameleon, it lives in dry forests and woodland. It lays up to 30 eggs in early winter. Although winter might seem a strange time to lay eggs, this is actually the dry season where this chameleon lives.

Chameleons

FIT TO DROP

Its short tail, brown pigmentation and dark lines make the West African leaf chameleon look like a dead leaf hanging from a twig. If disturbed it simply falls to the ground and lies still, blending in with the dead brown leaves on the forest floor. This small lizard reaches maturity in three months and feeds on termites, which it finds on the short rainforest shrubs where it lives.

DESERT DWELLER

Chameleons are usually associated with rainforest or woodland, but some species live in the desert. The Namaqua chameleon is found in the arid regions of Namibia and western South Africa. It spends most of its time on the ground but will climb on to rocks or into bushes to keep cool. The Namaqua chameleon has a large mouth and eats all kinds of animals, from insects to small lizards and snakes.

FAST DEVELOPERS

Natal dwarf chameleons live in dry thickets and gardens in South Africa. Males vary in appearance and may be bright blue or red. Females and juveniles are brown or green. The Natal chameleon gives birth to between eight and twenty live babies. These youngsters grow fast and can have babies of their own by the time they are nine months old. Such rapid development is a characteristic of many chameleons.

Hard Tongues

All lizards not contained in the Iguania belong to a group known as the Scleroglossa, or hard-tongued lizards. Their tongues are tough and flat. There are more than 2,700 species of hard-tongued lizard, ranging in size from the tiny insectivorous Caribbean least geckos to large carnivorous monitor lizards. Many of the 17 families have become burrowers and have lost their legs, after millions of years of them getting smaller and smaller to make burrowing easier. Hard-tongued lizards are the ancestors of amphisbaenians and snakes. They include a huge variety of species, among them geckos, lacertid lizards, zonures, skinks, anguid lizards and monitor lizards.

▲ STICKY FINGERS

Most geckos are nocturnal and hunt insects. The larger species, such as this tokay gecko, include other lizards in their diet. Geckos are best known for their ability to walk up walls and treetrunks and across ceilings. They do this with the aid of flattened toes with special plates called scansors on the underside. Not all geckos can climb like this, however.

SUN LOVERS ▶

Europe's eyed lizard preys on many smaller lizards, insects and spiders. Like most of the lizards that are commonly seen in Europe, it belongs to the lacertid family. Indeed the green lizards, wall lizards and ruin lizards often seen basking in the sun are all lacertids. The most widespread European species is the viviparous lizard. Other lacertids live in Africa and Asia. All lacertids are active and alert hunters of insects and spiders.

◄ **REAR GUARD**
The sungazer is the largest of the zonures, which are also called girdled lizards because their spiny scales are arranged in rings, or girdles, around the body. The sungazer has extremely spiny scales on its tail. The scales are used to defend the lizard when it dives head-first down a hole or wedges itself into a rocky crevice.

SMOOTHLY DOES IT ►
Most skinks, including this Müller's skink, have smooth shiny scales. Skinks make up the largest lizard family. Most skinks are small, active by day, live on the ground and eat insects. However, the Solomon's monkey-tail skink breaks all the rules by being a tree-living plant-eater that is active by night.

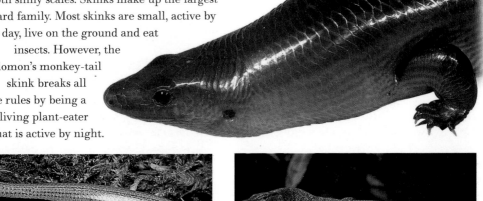

▲ WORM, SNAKE OR LIZARD?
The European slow-worm is a legless lizard. It feeds on slugs and other soft-bodied creatures. It is the best-known anguid lizard, but not all anguids lack limbs – the American alligator lizards have short legs, though they still wriggle along. The longest anguid is the 1m (3ft) European glass lizard. It looks like a snake but is a true lizard with eyelids and ear-openings.

▲ ALMOST INVISIBLE
This Indo-Malay water monitor is almost invisible against the rock it is lying on. Like other monitor lizards, it is a good climber and swimmer. They are found in Africa and Asia, but most live in Australia, and range in size from the 25cm (10in)-long short-tailed monitor to the giant Komodo dragon. Most eat insects or vertebrates but Gray's monitor also eats fruit.

139

Amphisbaenians

The amphisbaenians, also known as
worm-lizards, are a group of reptiles
that evolved from lizards. Worm-
lizards have tiny eyes covered by
transparent scales and rely mainly on
taste, smell and hearing to find their
way around. They are found in
Florida, the West Indies, Mexico,
South America, southern Europe, the
Middle East and Africa. Although
they are widely distributed, worm-
lizards are not very well understood
because they are rarely seen. Secretive
burrowers, they resemble earthworms.
Most species can discard their tails
when attacked, but they cannot grow
new ones, unlike many true lizards.
Most worm-lizards lay eggs, although a
few bear live young. All feed on soft-
bodied invertebrates, such as worms
and insect larvae (young).

▲ WHITE GIANT
The largest amphisbaenian is the white
worm-lizard of South America. It may
grow to a length of at least 55cm (22in)
and has a pointed snout and a blunt,
rounded tail. It hunts deep in the nests of
leaf-cutting ants. The white worm-lizard
follows ant trails back to the nest and
enters the refuse area deep below the ants'
carefully cultured fungus gardens. Once
there, it feeds on beetle larvae.

◀ ANT EATER
Black and white worm-lizards live in South
America in the Amazon rainforest. It is a large
species – like the white worm-lizard – and it can
reach up to 30cm (12in) in length. The black and
white worm-lizard's striking pattern contrasts
with its light pink head, which is usually marked
with a single central black spot. This species lives
in ant nests, where it lays its eggs, and feeds
mainly on ant larvae and pupae. It is seen above
ground only after heavy rain.

WEIRD AND WONDERFUL ▼

The ajolates, or mole worm-lizards, are among the strangest of all reptiles. Like other worm-lizards, they have elongated bodies covered with rings of small rectangular scales. The three known species of mole worm-lizards also have a pair of front feet for digging. Mole worm-lizards inhabit sandy low-lying country in Mexico. Their bodies have a long fold running from one end to the other. This fold may allow the body to expand when feeding or breathing.

◄ SOLE EUROPEAN

Europe's only amphisbaenian is the Iberian worm-lizard, which lives in Spain and Portugal. It has close relatives in Morocco. Usually black, brown or yellow in colour with a paler underside, and sometimes speckled with pink, at first sight this species looks like an earthworm. However, a closer examination will reveal a specialized, pointed head for burrowing, a mouth with a short tongue and tiny, faint eyes. The body is ringed with rows of tiny, square scales. Rarely seen above ground, this species is found under flat stones and in leaf-litter in sandy woodland and feeds on a wide variety of insects.

Did you know? In Greek myths the amphisbaenia was a monstrous snake with a head at each end.

◄ TUNNEL DIGGING

The chequered worm-lizard inhabits open rocky country and woodland in North Africa. It has a slightly pointed head and a stout body patterned with dark brown spots on a lighter background. When threatened, the chequered worm-lizard may roll into a ball. This species belongs to the most advanced family of worm-lizards, which have developed specialized techniques for tunnel excavation.

Where in the World

Lizards are the most numerous of all reptiles, and they are also among the most adaptable, living in regions where even snakes are absent. Lizards have adapted to cope with cold on mountains and inside the Arctic Circle and can endure the heat of any desert. They are excellent colonizers — especially those species that give birth to live young — able to adapt over time to feed on anything that is available. In fact, nearly everywhere you look on land, there is a good chance a lizard lives there. Unlike amphibians, which lived on Earth before reptiles, some lizards have learned to live in or near the sea and have adapted to deal with high levels of salt in their diets.

▲ DUSTY DESERT
Many lizards live in deserts but surviving there is hard. Desert lizards are often nocturnal to avoid the heat. They rarely drink, and many survive on the water they get from their food alone. Some desert lizards, such as this Namib gecko, have webbed feet or fringes on their toes to help them run over sand.

▲ ICY COLD
The Arctic is a far from ideal place for reptiles, but a few lizards do live in this cold region and are active in the short summers. The viviparous lizard is common throughout Europe but, unlike other European lizards, it is also found well inside the Arctic Circle. Viviparous means live-bearing, and most reptiles that live in cold climates give birth to live young.

▲ SEASHORE SALT
The swollen-snouted side-blotch lizard is one of the few lizards to live on the seashore. It lives on the tiny island of Isla Coloradito off Mexico where it eats shore-living crustaceans, called slaters, and the sea-lice that infest the sea-lion colony. The salt level in its diet is 20 times the lethal level of any other lizard. Special glands in its nostrils help it get rid of some of the salt.

◄ WHERE DO LIZARDS LIVE?

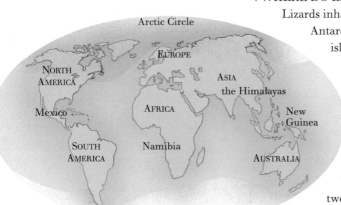

lizards live on
every continent
except the Antarctic

Lizards inhabit every continent apart from Antarctica and have colonized most island groups. Some species, such as house geckos, have even used human transport to reach and colonize islands a very long way from land. Lizards are not found in areas of very high altitude and latitude, because it is too cold for them. The five species shown on these two pages are from different continents and different habitats. The only things these lizards have in common is that they all survive in difficult conditions.

MOUNTAIN HIGH ►

The mountains are tough places for reptiles, which rely on the sun to keep them warm and active. Few lizards can survive in these conditions, but one exception is the rock agama from the southern Himalayas. It is found as high as 2,300m (7,500ft), basking on rocks along the freezing rivers that pour off the glaciers. It hibernates in winter to save energy and avoid the worst of the cold.

◄ STEAMY RAINFOREST

Lizards are everywhere in rainforests: in the canopy, on the tall trunks, down on the ground and underneath the leaf-litter. There is plenty of food in the forest but there are also plenty of predators so lizards have to be alert. New Guinea's twin crested anglehead lizard lives in rainforests but this particular lizard is seldom seen because it is well camouflaged.

143

A Marine

The marine iguana of the Galapagos Islands off Ecuador is the only truly ocean-going lizard in the world. It lives its entire life along the coast, never venturing far inland, and it survives on a diet of seaweed and the droppings of seals and crabs, which provides bacteria to aid its digestion. This diet results in dangerously high levels of salt entering the lizard's body. To avoid being poisoned, marine iguanas regularly get rid of the salt with loud snorts, spraying the white particles of salt on to the rocks, themselves and their neighbours. A typical day for a marine iguana is spent mostly basking in the sun and feeding.

SUNBATHERS

Basking is very important to marine iguanas, especially the males, which dive into the cold waters to feed. Without basking, they would be unable to warm up enough for their bodies to digest their food. Basking marine iguanas must be alert for predators. Snakes and birds of prey will kill small iguanas if they can catch them.

UNDERWATER BREAKFAST

Female and young marine iguanas forage for food on the exposed rocks at low tide, but the adult males are more adventurous. They dive into the water and swim down to the submerged seaweed beds to browse. Large males can dive as deep as 10m (33ft) in search of a meal.

HEAD TO HEAD

Male marine iguanas do not fall out over feeding grounds but they do disagree over mating territories. A mating territory is an area where an adult male has a good chance of meeting and courting females. These small patches of rock are disputed with body postures, head-bobs, gaping mouths and head-butting until one male gives in and leaves.

Iguana's Day

GROUP LIVING

Marine iguanas are unusual for large lizards, in that they gather together at night to sleep in groups, like sea lions. They even manage to sleep piled on top of one another. Marine iguanas are much less territorial than land iguanas, so fights do not break out over sleeping areas. By sleeping huddled together, they conserve energy and cool down more slowly than if they slept alone.

COURTSHIP FINERY

During the breeding season, the male marine iguana develops large patches of red, and sometimes green, skin, which contrasts strongly with his usual black or darker markings. At this time he is interested in mating with as many females as possible and spends a lot of his time trying to fend off smaller males and compete with larger males for mating territories.

ALL AT SEA

To get from one rocky outcrop to another, or to reach the deeper, richer feeding grounds, the marine iguana must venture into the sea. These lizards are extremely strong swimmers, powered by muscular tails, and this is essential because currents around the Galapagos are very strong.

Bone and Cartilage

The scaffolding that supports a lizard's body is called bone. This is a living tissue that develops as a lizard matures from juvenile to adult. In hatchlings the body is supported by flexible cartilage. As a lizard ages, calcium is deposited in the cartilage and it hardens, thickens and becomes bone. Lizards obtain calcium from their food. Different lizards have different skeletons and scientists have divided lizards into families based mostly on skeletal features and the way bones develop.

backbone

ribcage

skull

▲ LIZARD SKELETON

Most lizards have four legs, each ending in five toes. As with all reptiles, the body is supported by the backbone, which stretches from the neck to the tail. The backbone is actually not one bone but many small bones, or vertebrae. Important organs, such as the heart and lungs, are protected by the ribcage. The skull forms a tough case around the brain.

▼ IMPRESSIVE HEADGEAR

Many lizards have extra structures that stick out from their body. Johnston's chameleon has three large horns on the front of its head. The horns are made of soft tissue, and they grow from raised structures on the skull. All Johnston's chameleons have these horns but they are larger on males than females. Males use their horns to intimidate rivals and they may also be helpful in attracting a female mate.

▲ LOST LIMBS

Some lizards have fewer than five toes and others have lost their limbs altogether. Scaly-feet lizards have completely lost their front legs, and all that remains of their hind limbs is a small scaly flap. Despite the small size of the scaly flaps, they are used for grip when moving over rock.

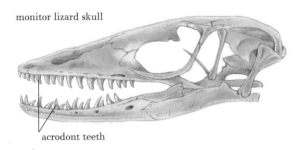

monitor lizard skull

monkeytail skink skull
(*not to scale*)

acrodont teeth

pleurodont teeth

▲ SKULL AND TEETH

Monitor lizards, chameleons, iguanas and agamas have their
teeth on top of the jawbone, which is known as acrodont. Other
lizards, such as the monkeytail skink, have pleurodont teeth,
positioned on the side of the jawbone. The lower jawbones are
linked to the back of the skull by a ball and socket joint.

Did you know? Many lizards are classified by the structure of the bones in their skull.

◄ DEFENSIVE UMBRELLA

When the Australian frilled lizard feels
threatened it opens its mouth. This
action causes a wide frill of skin
around its neck to open out like an
umbrella. The frill is supported
by special bones but is poorly
developed in juveniles. It is intended
to frighten an enemy and give the
lizard time to turn and run away. At rest,
or when the lizard is running or climbing,
the frill is folded along the body.

SPECIAL SAILS ►

Some lizards have a sail-like fin on their
back. Supported by cartilage or bony
extensions from the backbone, these
fins may serve more than one
purpose. In chameleons, they may
aid balance or help with camouflage
by making the lizard look more like
a leaf. They also increase a lizard's
body surface area to make it easier
to warm up quickly in the sun.

Internal Anatomy

Although on the outside, lizards look much like other living creatures, under the skin all kinds of peculiar anatomical adaptations help make them successful. Lizards have special breath-holding abilities, extra sensory organs and telescopic (extendable) tongues. A few species even have green blood to protect them from parasites. Internal anatomy covers everything beneath the skin, from the skeleton and muscles to the organs and blood. It includes not only the bones but also the muscles, tendons and ligaments that let the skeleton move, and soft-tissue organs such as the brain, thoracic and abdominal organs.

▲ TAKING A DIVE

When a green iguana basking over a river feels threatened, it may leap into the water, around 10m (30ft) below, swim to the bottom and stay there for up to 30 minutes. Iguanas are able to hold their breath and survive underwater like this by changing the flow of blood through the heart. Rather than sending blood from the body to the lungs, they can pump it back through the body and use up every bit of oxygen that is in it before they need to breathe again.

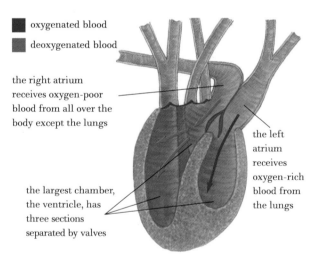

■ oxygenated blood

■ deoxygenated blood

the right atrium receives oxygen-poor blood from all over the body except the lungs

the left atrium receives oxygen-rich blood from the lungs

the largest chamber, the ventricle, has three sections separated by valves

▲ THREE-CHAMBERED HEART

A lizard's heart has three chambers, unlike ours, which has four. Two chambers, called the atria, receive blood from the body. Oxygen-rich blood from the left atrium is kept separate from oxygen-poor blood from the right.

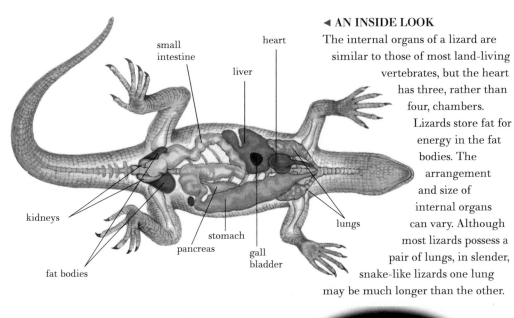

small
intestine

heart

liver

kidneys

stomach

pancreas

gall
bladder

lungs

fat bodies

◄ AN INSIDE LOOK

The internal organs of a lizard are similar to those of most land-living vertebrates, but the heart has three, rather than four, chambers. Lizards store fat for energy in the fat bodies. The arrangement and size of internal organs can vary. Although most lizards possess a pair of lungs, in slender, snake-like lizards one lung may be much longer than the other.

TONGUE AND GROOVES ►

Lizards' tongues begin at the front of their mouths, as can be seen in this photograph of a fat-tailed gecko's mouth. Mammals' tongues begin at the back of the throat. The open airway or glottis can be seen in the gecko's mouth. Forked-tongued lizards, such as monitors, have an extra organ, known as Jacobson's organ, which they use to analyse scent particles. The lizard places the tips of its tongue in two grooves in the roof of the mouth, which lead to the organ above.

◄ PROTECTIVE PIGMENT

Most lizards have red blood but one unusual group has blood that is green. Green-blooded skinks have a green pigment in their blood that would be poisonous to most animals. In the past it was thought that the skinks had this so that they would be unpleasant to eat. It is now believed the green pigment protects the skinks from blood parasites, such as the ones that cause malaria.

Skin and Scales

All reptiles have tough and almost entirely waterproof skin. Lizard skin is made up of three layers. The outer layer, or epidermis, is usually transparent and is shed, or sloughed, regularly as the lizard grows. Under the epidermis is a layer called the stratum intermediate, which contains the pigments. This gives the lizard its patterns. Beneath that is the inner layer, or dermis. In many hard-tongued lizards, this layer contains rigid plates known as osteoderms (bone skin), which add strength to the skin. Scales vary greatly in shape and texture from the smooth, rounded scales of skinks to the sharp, keeled (ridged) scales of zonures. Lizards do not have sweat glands as mammals do, but they have special glands between the scales.

▲ PROTECTIVE PLATES
Plated lizards, such as this southern African rough-scaled plated lizard, possess rectangular plate-like scales arranged in regular overlapping rows around the body. These scales are strengthened by the presence of protective osteoderms (bony plates). Along each of the lizard's flanks is a long fold of skin containing small granular scales. This enables the plated lizard to expand its body when it breathes, in what would otherwise be a very constricting hard shell.

SMOOTH AND SHINY ▶
This slow-worm and many ground-dwelling skinks have bodies covered in small, rounded, smooth scales that offer little resistance when the reptile is burrowing or moving underneath debris. The slow-worm is legless so when it sheds its epidermis, the entire layer often comes off in one large piece, not inside out like a snake. The skin of the slow-worm contains protective osteoderms.

▲ TINY BEADS

The Salvador's monitor lizard, which is a large tree-climbing lizard from New Guinea, has numerous tiny scales. The smaller and more regular a lizard's scales are, the more flexible its body is. The Gila monster and beaded lizard have scales that look even more like beads.

▲ MOBILE FOLDS

The small scales of South America's northern tegu are arranged in a series of overlapping triangular folds. The northern tegu is a speedy hunter, and this arrangement of scale-groups moving over one another as the lizard runs gives the tegu both protection and agility.

▲ SHARP RIDGES

The back of the Bosc monitor lizard from the African savannas has numerous interlocking but non-overlapping keeled scales. Those on the lizard's underside are smaller and not keeled. Keeled scales may help dew condense on the lizard's back at night, giving it water to drink in an otherwise arid environment.

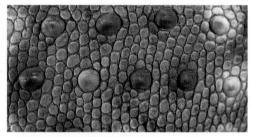

▲ SCATTERED SCALES

Geckos have granular, velvety or papery skin. The tokay gecko has scattered conical scales surrounded by smaller, granular scales. The skin of smaller geckos is usually much more fragile. One species from Madagascar sheds all three layers of its skin if grasped.

OFF WITH THE OLD ▶

Lizards must shed the outer layer of their skins in order to grow. Unlike snakes, they tend to shed their skin in pieces. This wonder gecko has begun to shed its old skin. Since the cells that produce patterns are in the second layer, the old skin looks clear. The original patterns are visible in the newly emerged gecko.

151

How Lizards

BROKEN GLASS

Many lizards are able to lose their tails for protection. This Australian scaly-foot has a long tail that can be quickly discarded if grasped. The European slow-worm got its scientific name *Anguis fragilis* from the fact that it is easily 'broken'. The scheltopusik got its other name, glass snake, because it is legless and has the habit of breaking its extremely long tail.

Small lizards often show their tails when threatened. Some species have brightly patterned tails that, combined with a tail-waving motion, attract a predator's attention and draw its attack away from the lizard's head and body. As a predator pounces on the lizard's tail, powerful muscular contractions in the tail cause it to snap off. The discarded tail then thrashes around, so that the predator's attention is further distracted and the lizard can escape. The muscles at the severance point collapse to seal the end of the tail and prevent blood loss. The wound soon heals and the lizard grows a new tail.

broken tail

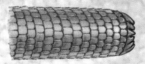

new tail

TAIL INTACT

The common house gecko has many enemies that would like to make a meal of it. This gecko has been lucky — it still has its original tail but would be prepared to sacrifice it in an instant if threatened by a predator. The original tail is patterned like the body and has different scales on the top from those underneath.

THE ESCAPE MECHANISM

Lizards that can lose their tails have special breaking points built into them. When the tail is grasped, powerful muscular contractions will cause a fracture right through the tail, severing it at that point. The muscles then close the wound preventing further loss of blood.

Grow New Tails

A LOST TAIL

A lizard may try to escape capture by losing its tail. At first, this house gecko's tail thrashes about vigorously but it is now still, and lying upside down. Since the muscle bundles in the injured base of the tail have collapsed to seal the wound, there has been little blood loss. Although the gecko may look strange without its tail, at least it is still alive and can escape from its enemy. It has survived its ordeal and can carry on life as before. Over time, a new tail will grow to replace the one that it has lost.

NEARLY AS GOOD AS NEW

This house gecko lost its tail some time ago and has now grown a new one. The new tail is supported not by bone but by a rod of cartilage – the same material you have in the bridge of your nose. The new tail does not look as good as the old one, it looks like a cheap add-on part, but it does the job almost as well as the original.

A LIZARD WITH TWO TAILS

When a lizard loses only part of its tail, it can grow what is called a bifurcated tail. This house gecko escaped, with the original tail loosely attached to the body. Since the blood vessels survived, the original tail recovered. But another tail grew out from the open wound, resulting in a curious fork-tailed gecko.

Getting Around

The typical lizard has four well-developed legs, each with five clawed toes. The legs stick out from the side of the body. This means that the body is thrown into S-shaped curves when the lizard walks or runs. Lizard backbones are flexible to let the lizard move easily as its stride lengthens. Some lizards run very fast on all fours. Others run even more quickly using just their hind legs with the front of the body raised and the tail for balance. In tree-dwelling species the feet and tail may be adapted for climbing.

▲ SPIDER-MEN
Geckos are famous for their ability to run up walls and glass, but not all geckos can do this. Only the geckos with expanded digits, such as house geckos and tokay geckos, can climb sheer surfaces. Under their toes are a series of flattened plates called 'scansors', which mean they can stick on to almost any flat surface.

▼ WALKING ON WATER
Basilisks escape predators by running very fast on their long-toed hind-limbs. They can sprint across water for quite a way before they break the surface of the water and fall in. This unusual ability to run on water has earned them the nickname of 'Jesus lizard'. Some other long-legged lizards can also run on water.

▲ A FIFTH LIMB
Some tree-living lizards have prehensile tails, which they can use when climbing. The monkey-tail skink is a large lizard from the Solomon Islands that uses its powerful tail when clambering in the forest canopy.

▲ LEAP FOR FREEDOM

Flying lizards and flying geckos do not actually fly but glide down from trees to avoid predators. The flying gecko has webs of skin between its toes and also along the side of its body to slow its descent, but this flying lizard is more elaborate. It has a pair of 'wings' spread out by false ribs to produce the lizard equivalent of a parachute.

▲ LIFE UNDERGROUND

Many desert lizards spend part of their lives underground, escaping there from enemies or the heat of the sun. Africa's sand fish disappears into loose sand extremely rapidly, digging with its legs and flattened snout. Other lizards have developed an elongated body and lost their limbs so that they can swim through the sand like eels in water.

Night Fighters

'Gecko' is an onomatopoeic word – a word that sounds like what it describes. This comes from the Malay word 'gekok', which is derived from the noise that some geckos make when they call. The tokay gecko has another call which sounds like 'tow-kay'. Geckos are active after dark, and this led the Japanese to give the name 'Gekkoh' to their night-fighter aircraft in World War II.

HOLDING ON ▶

Chameleons' toes are fused together. Each foot has three toes opposing two toes. The toes grip in the same way as a human's opposing thumb and other four fingers. This makes the chameleon such an expert climber that it can walk along slender twigs.

155

Sensing the Surroundings

Lizards have a variety of finely tuned sense organs to enable them to move around, locate and capture prey, avoid predators and find a mate. Eye-sight is an important sense for most lizards but the structure of the retina (the back of the inside of the eye) varies greatly. The retinas of day-living lizards are dominated by cells called cones, giving them detailed vision, while those of nocturnal species have far more light-sensing rod cells, increasing their ability to see by moonlight. Lizards that are active at dusk and dawn have vertical pupils that close down to protect the sensitive retina from bright daylight. Day-living lizards may also possess detailed vision.

▲ EAGLE EYES

Lizards that are active by day, such as the green iguana, have excellent vision. Focusing for studying close detail is accomplished by changing the shape of the soft, deformable lens of the eye. Many lizards need to be able to focus rapidly because they move around quickly and with agility so that they can catch fast-moving insects. Vision is also important for basking lizards as they must be able to spot approaching predators.

◄ LOOKING TWO WAYS AT ONCE

Chameleons are the only land vertebrates with eyes that move independently. This Parson's chameleon can use its turret-eyes to look in two directions at the same time as it seeks out prey. When an insect is located, both eyes converge on the prey and, working like a telephoto lens, they focus quickly and precisely to enlarge the image. The turret eyes and the long sticky tongue evolved to work together, making chameleons expert shots when they shoot out their tongues to capture insects.

▼ A THIRD EYE

Green iguanas and many other lizards have a small circular object in the centre of their heads. This is the pineal eye, a third eye with a lens, retina and a nerve feeding back into the brain, but it has no muscles, making it unable to focus. The pineal eye may help basking lizards to monitor how much sunlight they are receiving but the way in which it works is not yet fully understood.

▲ LISTENING LIZARDS

Lizard ears are made up of three parts: the outer, middle and inner ear. The eardrum of this bearded dragon is clearly visible on the side of its head because the outer ear is absent. In other species the eardrum is hidden by a deep outer ear opening. Most lizards have external ears but some have scales over them and others have no eardrum at all.

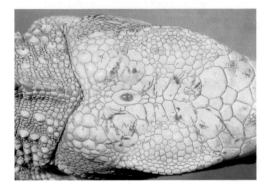

SEEK WITH FORKED TONGUE ▶

Some hard-tongued lizards have a Jacobson's organ that allows them to 'taste' the air and track prey from a long way away. The forked tongue of this water monitor lizard is picking up scent particles and delivering them to the Jacobson's organ to be analysed. The forks of the tongue help it tell direction – if more interesting particles are on the right fork the lizard turns right.

◀ PECULIAR TASTES

The herbivorous monkey-tail skink has a bulbous tongue with a slightly bi-lobed tip that contains many taste buds. This skink does not eat insects or meat so it does not have to track down any prey, but probably uses its sensitive tongue to discriminate between suitable and unsuitable leaves. Monkey-tail skinks are social lizards, and tongue-licking may also be a way of recognizing other members of the colony.

157

The Carnivores

Although the majority of lizards are either partly or entirely carnivorous (meat-eating), even plant-eating lizards will occasionally eat insects. Many lizards are active predators, hunting down their prey and capturing it with a lightning dash. Some meat-eating lizards take advantage of wounded, sick, dying or dead animals for an easy meal. Animals that feed like this are called scavengers. Many lizards have a strong sense of smell and are able to locate prey that is hidden or buried. Komodo dragons are able to smell prey from up to 4km (2½ miles) away. Other monitor lizards, and tegus, are experts at finding the eggs of turtles, crocodiles and other lizards.

▲ **MANY MINI MEALS**

Ants are very small prey but some lizards specialize in eating them. The horned lizards of North America's deserts are squat spiny lizards that feed entirely on ants. Because ants are small, hundreds must be eaten at each meal. Fortunately for horned lizards, ants occur in large numbers and swarm together when their colony is attacked.

▲ **PINPOINT ACCURACY**

A chameleon, such as this panther chameleon, approaches its insect prey with stealth, focusing both eyes on the insect to judge how far away it is and extending its head forwards as it gauges the moment to strike. Once the lizard is in position, it shoots out its long tongue rapidly and then pulls it back into its mouth with the insect stuck on the tip. Chameleons have prehensile tails, adapted for grasping, which help them grip on to twigs and branches when they are hunting.

Did you know? The chameleon's tongue is so long that it may be twice the length of its entire body.

▼ CRUSHING BITE

The swamp-dwelling caiman lizard from the Amazon rainforest looks a little like a crocodile. An excellent swimmer, it hunts aquatic snails underwater. These are crushed between flat teeth in the caiman lizard's powerful jaws.

▲ DOWN IN ONE

Most legless lizards have tiny mouths and can eat only small prey. But Burton's snake-lizard, a relative of Australia's geckos, specializes in eating skinks. Its jaws are much more flexible than those of other lizards and its teeth curve backwards, allowing it to swallow prey whole and head first in the same way as a snake does.

◄ FEARLESS KILLER

Most monitor lizards are true all-round carnivores, feeding on small mammals, scavenging the carcasses of lion kills and stealing eggs from crocodile nests. Unlike most other animals, large monitors are not even afraid of snakes, and often feed on them. This Nile monitor is killing a sand snake, which is helpless against the monitor lizard's crushing jaws.

DANGEROUS PREY ►

Some lizards feed on very dangerous prey. North African desert agamas usually eat harmless insects but sometimes they make a meal of a scorpion. To do this it must act quickly, and crush the scorpion in its powerful jaws before its tail can deliver its deadly sting.

Vegetarian Lizards

Plant-eating reptiles are rare, and only tortoises, and a few turtles and lizards, have a truly vegetarian diet. Many lizards that eat vegetation also eat insects and so are really omnivores (animals that eat plants and meat). Some lizards start life eating insects and only turn vegetarian as they become adults. Most plant-eating lizards feed on leaves, which are easy to find but hard to digest. Many leaf-eating lizards select only fresh, new shoots, which are easier to digest. Eating fruit is easier but less common in lizards, and a few species feed on seeds, flower heads or nectar. One lizard, the marine iguana, eats seaweed.

▲ BLOOMING TASTY

The San Esteban spiny-tailed iguana lives on an arid island in the Mexican Sea of Cortez and eats cactus flowers and other plants. Iguanas are the main group of leaf-eating lizards, but there may be few leaves in arid habitats, and desert island iguanas often feed on the flowers and fruit of cacti and other water-retaining succulents.

◄ SALTY FOOD

The Galapagos marine iguana is the only truly marine lizard. While its two Galapagos land iguana relatives have a rich diet of leaves and flowers, the male marine iguana must enter into the cold ocean to feed. Marine iguanas dive down to 10m (33ft) to feed on seaweed before returning to bask on the rocks. There is so much salt in their food that they have special glands in their nostrils to get rid of it.

▼ FRUITY FEAST

This little Barbados anole is enjoying a feast of bruised mango fruit. Feeding on fruit is a much easier option than eating leaves. Fruit is easily digested, and it provides much more energy than leaves. However, fruit is seasonal, so lizards that like to eat fruit have to be prepared to eat other things as well, such as insects.

▲ VEG GIANT

Although most monitor lizards are meat-eaters, one species eats fruit more than anything else. Gray's monitor lizard from the Philippines habitually swallows whole fruit and is the world's only plant-eating monitor lizard. It also eats insects but fruit can make up almost 60 per cent of its diet. Other lizards, including the iguanas and chuckwallas of the Americas, eat leaves. Digesting leaves requires a large, specialized gut with valves to slow down the passage of leaves through the digestive system.

▼ DRIED-OUT DIET

Lizards living in very dry deserts have little green vegetation available to eat. They bulk out their insect diets by feeding on seeds in the dry season when insects are scarce. In the arid Namib Desert of south-western Africa, the shovel-snouted lizard is perfectly able to survive on wind-blown seeds alone. It obtains not only its energy but also all of its water requirements from this incredibly dry diet.

Did you know? Some lizards eat insects when young, then move to a diet of leaves as they get older.

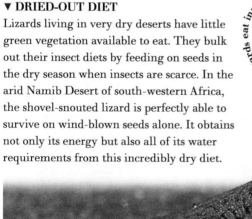

Focus on the

The Komodo dragon, or Ora as it is also known, is the largest lizard in the world and the only one believed to include humans in its diet. The size of the dragon has been exaggerated however – the maximum length for the dragon is not much more than 3m (10ft) – and attacks on humans are very rare. The Komodo dragon is a type of monitor lizard that is confined to four small islands in Indonesia's Komodo group. It has one of the smallest geographical ranges of any of the large carnivores, and is classified as endangered. Komodo dragons feed mainly on large animals, such as deer, which they attack by ambush. Once bitten, the prey is doomed to die, even if it escapes. The Komodo dragon's saliva contains deadly bacteria that cause death through blood poisoning within a couple of days.

HUMAN PREY?
This is a view from Baron's Cross on Komodo Island. The Baron's Cross commemorates the Swiss naturalist, Baron Rudolph von Reding, who disappeared on the island in 1974, having strayed away from his tour group. No one knows for certain how he died, but all that was left of him were his glasses and camera, on the hill where the Baron's Cross now stands.

IN THE TREETOPS
The first thing a newly hatched Komodo dragon does is run for the nearest tree and climb quickly up it. Young Komodo dragons live in the treetops for two years, safe from the adults, who live on the ground. The young eat large insects, geckos and skinks.

Komodo Dragon

FIRST TO ARRIVE

Komodo dragons have an extremely good sense of smell and they can detect prey from a long distance. This large adult dragon on Rinca Island has been attracted by the smell of a dead goat. The lizard has powerful jaws and its muscular legs are armed with talon-like claws, enabling it to rip prey open and devour it very quickly.

THREE'S A CROWD

Two more, slightly smaller, dragons arrive. Soon after this picture was taken a fight broke out. Eventually the largest dragon took the goat by the head and started to bolt down almost the entire carcass, while the other two ripped pieces of flesh away. Less than 20 minutes later, the goat had completely disappeared.

ARTIFICIAL GATHERING

In the past, park rangers used to attract Komodo dragons to a feeding station so that tourists could safely watch them. This practice is no longer carried out since the dragons were becoming reliant on the handouts and were beginning to think of tourists as a source of food. The dragons now act naturally again and seek out their own food.

163

▲ LAPPING IT UP

Many lizards drink by lapping up water with their tongues. This Madagascan day gecko has climbed down a tree in order to drink from a puddle. Northern Madagascar, where this day gecko lives, is quite a wet region, with regular rainfall. For the majority of lizards, finding water to drink is not a problem.

Water for Life

Like all animals, lizards need water to survive. They obtain it in several ways, depending on the species and habitat. Many drink water from pools or puddles, or get it from dewdrops or condensed fog. Moisture can also be obtained from food. For some lizards, finding water is hard, and a few never drink at all. Lizards living in very dry places produce harder, drier droppings than those in rainforests, where water is in plentiful supply. This helps them conserve water that would otherwise be wasted. Some lizards use water produced inside their own bodies. 'Metabolic' water is created when food is broken down within the body. A few desert-adapted specialists use this 'metabolic water' so that they do not need to drink.

▲ WATERPROOF COAT

This Bell's dab lizard is basking in the sun. If an amphibian or mammal did this, it would lose a lot of water, either from its moist skin or by sweating, but lizards have tough, dry skin that keeps most water in. This is one reason why reptiles are so common in hot, dry places.

SHADY CHARACTER ▶

The ornate tree lizard lives on large trees along riverbanks in the south-west of the USA. These trees have rough bark and broad leaves, which provide lots of shade. Rainfall is rare in this area, so the lizard must get all the water that it needs from its insect prey. An ornate tree lizard has to eat seven or eight insects a day to get enough water to survive.

Stony Stare of the Basilisk

According to mythology, the basilisk's stare could turn people to stone or cause them to burst into flame. Also known as the Cockatrice or Royal Serpent, this mythological basilisk is shown as a type of dragon, sometimes as a snake-like creature, as in Harry Potter and the Chamber of Secrets. *No one knows what the mythological basilisk looked like because anyone who saw one would never speak again! Real basilisks are harmless Central American lizards whose main claim to fame is that they can run across water.*

▲ DEVIL'S DEW

The thorny devil comes from the deserts of western Australia, where it hardly ever rains. But the thorny devil's diet of ants does not provide it with enough water to survive. The lizard gets around this problem by drinking any dew that condenses on its body at night. The dew trickles down channels between its 'thorns' and into the corner of its mouth.

◄ OUT IN THE SUN

The western brush lizard is closely related to the ornate tree lizard but it lives in the sparse bushes and trees of the Sonoran Desert. With their small leaves and slender branches, these bushes offer little shade from the sun. The brush lizard loses much more water than the tree lizard and must eat 11 or 12 insects a day to keep its water levels topped up.

▼ WATER FROM FAT

Some desert geckos, such as Australia's Kimberley fringe-toed velvet gecko, store fat in their tails to help them survive. This fat is mainly used to provide energy when food is short, but it can be broken down to make water. One gram of fat produces just over one gram of water.

165

Body Temperature

A lizard's body temperature depends on the temperature of its surroundings. Unlike birds or mammals, which produce their own body heat, cold-blooded lizards need to bask on hot surfaces such as sun-heated rock or have warm air around them. In the hot tropics, lizards can be active day or night. Elsewhere, they need the heat of the sun to raise their body temperature. Most lizards speed up this process by basking. Although they need the sun, lizards must be careful not to get too hot.

▲ ON GUARD

A lizard in the sun has to keep its eyes open for predators. Birds of prey are a particular threat to this African ground agama — the slightest shadow will send it dashing back to its refuge, a hole at the base of the bush. A basking lizard may look like a dozing sunbather, but it will usually be alert.

▲ TOO HOT TO HANDLE

If you have ever walked barefoot on sand in the summer you know how hot it can be. Desert lizards have to deal with this problem every day. The African ground agama gets around it by standing on the balls of its feet. Other species do a balancing act, standing on two feet with two raised, before swapping over.

◄ SUN-POWERED

Some male lizards appear very bright to attract a female. The male common agama is bright blue and red, but only during the daytime. At night the sleeping lizard is much drabber and duller, but it rapidly becomes much brighter as it warms up. After a minute or so of basking in the sun, the lizard changes from brown to glowing red and blue again.

▲ BASKING IN THE RAINFOREST

Not much sunlight reaches the ground in a rainforest, yet some lizards warm up by basking on the rainforest floor. When a rainforest tree falls, it creates a natural gap in the canopy, and a patch of sunlight appears on the ground. In tropical America, ameivas seek out these sunny patches, and are usually the first lizards to arrive after a tree has fallen.

▲ WARM AT NIGHT

Lizards that hunt at night still need to be warm to be active. The granite night lizard from California spends the day in a rocky crevice, venturing forth to capture insects and scorpions only after dark. It manages to do this by seeking out spots where the rocks are still warm from the sun's rays. It is also able to remain active at temperatures too low for most lizards.

CATCHING THE RAYS ▶

So that they can warm up quickly, basking lizards flatten themselves to expose as much of their bodies to the sun or the warm ground. They do this by expanding their ribs outwards and making themselves more rounded. Some desert lizards are naturally rounded and can present almost half their body surface to the sun.

ON TIPTOES ▶

This northern desert horned lizard is round and flattened – the ideal shape for basking since it can present a large surface area to the sun. When it gets too hot, it lifts the underside of its body and tail off the sand so that it does not burn. Horned lizards spend long periods of time almost motionless, waiting for the ants that they feed on to swarm into reach.

Mating Time

In nearly every lizard species the male courts the female rather than the other way around. Male lizards go to great lengths to attract a mate and often put themselves in danger as a result. Some become brighter while others change the way they behave making themselves as obvious to predators as to females. Male lizards may even go without eating as the urge to mate or defend a female overrides their hunger for food. Males of most lizard species will mate with more than one female if they get the chance. Very few lizards stay with one partner through a mating season, though some Australian shingleback skinks stay together for life. A few lizard species do not need males to reproduce, and females of these species produce offspring without the need to mate.

▲ GIVING THE NOD

Male green iguanas use the dewlaps hanging down from their chins to settle disputes over mating territories. The dewlap is green, but dominant males develop a paler looking head and orange pigment on their shoulders. The dewlap draws attention to the signature bob display.

◀ WAVING A FLAG

Anole lizards are well camouflaged from predators but have a trick that makes them obvious when they want to attract a mate. Anoles possess a brightly patterned throat flag, or dewlap, which remains hidden until erected for display. Different species have different patterned dewlaps so that males do not attract females of the wrong species.

▲ PUTTING ON A SHOW

In many species of lizard the males develop brightly patterned skin to attract females during the breeding season. The European sand lizard is a good example since the males become bright green on the flanks in spring and summer while the females remain brown.

▼ TEST OF STRENGTH

If a visual display fails to deter a rival, some of the larger lizards, such as these Gould's monitor lizards, will resort to brute force. Fights between male monitors look aggressive as they rear up and try to grapple each other to the ground, but it is rare for either combatant to be injured. Instead, the defeated lizard will break away from the fight and run off.

◄ DANGEROUS LIAISONS

Once a male lizard has courted a female and chased off any rivals, he will try to mate with her. In the early stages he rubs his chin on her neck or nudges her until she lifts her tail and allows him to mate. Some animals, such as these Californian alligator lizards, may mate for a long time, so the female looks out to spot enemies.

VIRGIN BIRTH ►

Some lizards can produce offspring without mating. When this happens, the babies are identical clones of their mother. Lizards that can give birth without mating include the Indo-Pacific house gecko. Such species are good colonizers of islands, since a single arrival can start a colony all on her own.

169

Egg Layers

Most lizards lay eggs, but a significant minority, particularly in colder climates, give birth to live young. Although most egg-laying lizards lay eggs with soft, leathery shells, some geckos lay eggs with hard shells like those of birds. Few lizards show interest in their eggs or young, generally leaving after laying or giving birth. Some larger species, however, such as iguanas or monitor lizards, may guard the nest site for a short time after laying. Baby lizards are independent from birth or hatching. As soon as they are born they face a wide range of predators and few juveniles survive to adulthood.

▲ SPOTTED MOTHER

Leopard geckos inhabit grassland from Iran to India. A female leopard gecko can breed at the age of two and continue to breed for 14 years. Females lay two leathery-shelled eggs one month after mating. A female may produce eight clutches (16 eggs) in a year, potentially producing over 160 eggs in her life.

◄ BEFORE LAYING

Eggs can be seen in the body of this female house gecko. Most lizards lay eggs rather than give birth to live young. Geckos have clutches of only one or two eggs. Pale areas in the gecko's neck contain a substance called calcium carbonate, which is used to strengthen the eggshell before the eggs are laid.

INDEPENDENT BABY ▶

Hatchling leopard geckos measure 8–9cm (3–3½in) and have a much bolder ringed pattern than the adults. During its first few days, the baby survives on its absorbed yolk reserves. When these reserves run out, it will start to hunt for insects.

SOFT-SHELLED EGGS ▶

The eggs of most lizards have soft, leathery shells, and they are vulnerable to drying out, so they are usually laid in moist sand or soil. Hatching lizards break out using a small 'egg tooth' in the front of the mouth, which drops off soon after the lizard has hatched. This newly emerging collared lizard will survive for days on the absorbed contents of its yolk sac before it needs to hunt insects.

◀ MAKING A BREAK FOR IT

Unlike the hard-shelled eggs of most other geckos, leopard gecko eggs have leathery shells. After 6–12 weeks the infant gecko is ready to hatch. It cuts a small hole in the eggshell using a small egg tooth on the front of its jaw. Once it has absorbed the last of the yolk from its yolk sac and learned how to breathe using its lungs, it breaks out of the shell.

Did you know? A baby lizard's egg tooth drops off soon after it has slit a hole in the egg and hatched.

HARD PROTECTION ▶

Tree-living geckos, such as the gold dust day gecko, lay only a pair of eggs. At the moment they are laid they are soft and will fit into crevices in bark or on walls, sticking to both surfaces and the other egg. The eggs harden quickly when they come into contact with the air, giving the developing babies protection from drying out.

Birth and Hatching

Some species of lizards lay eggs while others give birth to live young. Female lizards who give birth carry their offspring for less time than a female who lays eggs. Most lizards in warm climates lay eggs, but those living in colder habitats, such as Scandinavia, Patagonia or Tasmania, usually give birth to live young. Such females can protect their young. They can seek out the sun and avoid enemies until the babies are ready to be born. Once born, their mother rarely takes care of them. Whether they are born or hatch from eggs, the juvenile lizards exist for a short time on the nutrients absorbed from the yolk sac, but they must soon become predators of insects and other small animals, or they will be eaten by larger creatures than themselves.

▲ LIVE YOUNG
About one in five lizard species give birth to live young. The babies are born wrapped in thin, transparent sacs from which they soon escape, taking a first breath in the process. Many live-bearing lizards live where it would be too cold for eggs to incubate. The common lizard has live young and lives as far north as Scandinavia inside the Arctic Circle.

◀ PROTECTIVE MOTHER
Only one lizard guards its young, the Solomons monkey-tail skink. Females usually give birth to a single infant, which never strays far from its mother and will seek shelter underneath her if it is threatened. Since the skink is a plant-eater, it is important that the baby eats some of its mother's droppings to obtain the microbes needed for it to digest leaves.

▲ GIVING BIRTH

Adult common lizards mate from March to June depending on their location. The embryos take up to three months to develop inside the female, and she gives birth to a single litter between July and September. The average size of a litter is seven or eight, but large females may give birth to up to 11 offspring. The babies are born in a membranous sac from which they escape within seconds. In warmer parts of the world, the common lizard may lay eggs. All baby common lizards have an egg tooth, even those that are born rather than laid in eggs.

Beware of Lizards
Iguanas might look cute when they are small, but these little green lizards can grow to 2m (6ft) in length. All iguanas need to have special lighting and follow a special diet if they are to keep healthy. When they are three years old, male green iguanas may become quite aggressive in the breeding season, biting and using the tail as a whip. Female iguanas often become eggbound in captivity because they have not been allowed to mate and lay eggs. An eggbound lizard may die. You should never buy a lizard on impulse or because it looks cute. Even baby Komodo dragons look cute – but they have a nasty bite.

Did you know? Green iguanas guard their eggs to stop others digging them up and laying their own.

▲ FAST WARM UP

Baby common lizards measure just under 4cm (1½in) long. They are independent from birth and must find their own food and avoid numerous predators if they are to survive to adulthood. In Britain, newborn common lizards are much darker than adults. They may even be black, which helps them warm up faster in the sun in order to hunt and be alert enough to avoid being captured.

Lizards under Attack

Snakes, birds of prey and mammals such as mongooses and meerkats are all enemies of lizards, and they are capable of catching even the most alert, fast-moving species by day or night. More unusual predators include other lizards and various large invertebrates including spiders, scorpions and centipedes. Many predators are opportunistic and include lizards as only part of their diet. But others are more specialized and regularly prey on them — snakes in particular. Lizards have evolved all sorts of ways of escaping from predators but the main reason that they survive as species is that they are simply so abundant. A single lizard can have dozens of offspring in a lifetime, and only a few of those offspring have to survive long enough to breed for the species to continue.

▲ **STRENGTH IN NUMBERS**

A single army ant would be a small snack for most lizards but a swarm of army ants is another story. These fierce insects march across the rainforest floor in South America and overpower anything that gets in their way. Most of their prey is made up of other insects but sometimes they kill and eat small lizards, too.

◄ **EIGHT-LEGGED ENEMY**

Invertebrates are animals without a backbone. Many species of lizards feed on invertebrates but sometimes large invertebrates turn the tables and make the lizards their prey. In many parts of the world, arachnids such as scorpions and large spiders hunt and kill small lizards. This wheel spider is eating a web-footed gecko that it has caught among the dunes of south-west Africa's Namib desert.

◄ EATING EACH OTHER

A few lizards specialize in eating other lizards. For example, the slender pygopodid snake-lizards are specialist predators of skinks. In the deserts of North America small spiny lizards are the main prey of larger lizard species. Here a black-collared lizard has caught a spiny lizard that was basking among the rocks.

CAUGHT UP IN THE COILS ►

A huge number of snakes prey on lizards and some feed on very little else. The common Asian wolf snake is one species that specializes in hunting lizards. Active at night, often inside houses, it will search underneath baskets, boxes or boards for small lizards, which are then grabbed and constricted before they are eaten. This wolf snake has a house gecko in its coils.

◄ DEATH FROM ABOVE

A few birds, such as secretary birds and the kookaburra, specialize in killing and eating snakes and lizards. Many other birds, including this black-shouldered kite from Namibia, will eat any basking lizard that is not paying attention to the threat from the skies. Small lizards will be swallowed head first and whole, while larger ones are torn apart by beak and claw to be eaten in chunks.

STRAIGHT FOR THE HEAD ►

The reptile-eating habits of some mammals are well known. Meerkats are small members of the same family as the cobra-killing mongooses. Smaller than a mongoose, the meerkat feeds on roots and small animals, including lizards. The meerkat's long canine teeth make short work of lizards, especially since the head is targeted first.

Avoiding Enemies

▲ BOLD DISPLAY
The toad-headed agama of Iran and southern Russia puts on a bold display. When threatened, it raises the front of its body, opens its mouth wide and extends flaps at either side to make it look threatening. It then hisses, waves its tail like a scorpion, and jumps towards its enemy.

Many lizards are small and looked upon as food by other animals. To escape being eaten, lizards have evolved a wide array of defensive mechanisms. One of the most effective is simply being well camouflaged and staying still to avoid detection. When this fails, the lizard may have to adopt a more active method of defending itself. Running away, diving off a branch or even gliding to freedom are all simple escape procedures. But many lizards have evolved more elaborate ways to defend themselves, including displays intended to intimidate or confuse potential predators. Some of these are among the most extreme seen anywhere in the animal kingdom.

◄ PUTTING ON A SHOW
The Australian frilled lizard's first reaction to danger is to open its mouth wide to spread its neck frill. All of this makes the lizard seem suddenly less like an easy meal and more a large, dangerous opponent. If this display fails to scare off a predator, the lizard turns tail and runs, the frill trailing around its neck like a partially closed umbrella. The frilled lizard uses its display to scare rivals as well as predators.

THREATENING DISPLAY ▶

The shingleback skink from Australia tries to frighten predators by opening its mouth and sticking out its bright blue tongue. These lizards have short legs so they cannot run away and must stand their ground. The rolling tongue, combined with a flattening and curving of the body, and a hiss, is enough to intimidate most animals.

▲ SEEING RED

The horned lizards of Mexico and the USA have one of the strangest mechanisms to warn off predators – they squirt foul-tasting blood from the corners of their eyes. They use this only against large predators. Birds and rodents are usually seen off by the lizard's prickly spines.

▼ FIGHTING TINY ENEMIES

New Guinea's green-blooded skinks have a pigment in their blood that makes it bright green. This is to defend against the tiny blood parasites that cause a disease called malaria. Lizards suffer from seven types of malaria. The skinks' blood is believed to be so toxic the malarial parasite cannot survive.

▼ CHAMPION WRESTLER

Monitor lizards have powerful jaws, which can deliver a painful bite. They use their tails as whips, dealing rapid blows to their enemies. When the argus monitor is threatened, it makes itself look bigger by standing on its hind feet and inflating its throat. If this fails, it attacks, wrestling fiercely until its opponent flees.

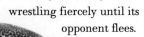

Did you know? The frilled lizard can run on its back legs at speeds of more than 20kph (12½ mph).

Patterns and Camouflage

A lizard's appearance is usually dictated by the habitat in which it lives: most desert lizards are sandy brown, most tree-living species are bark-brown or green. By matching themselves to their background they become well camouflaged, which protects them from animals that want to eat them. Some lizards take camouflage one step further and actually look like objects from their surroundings. Changing appearance is also important socially. Male lizards may adopt a bright appearance in the mating season, or expose bright parts of the body when confronted by a rival.

▲ **DEAD LEAF**
Not all chameleons are green or camouflaged like living leaves. The West African pygmy chameleon lives in low vegetation in forests and is a drab brown with a series of darker lines making it look like a dead leaf. When the pygmy chameleon feels threatened, it simply falls to the forest floor and lies still, disappearing among the leaf-litter.

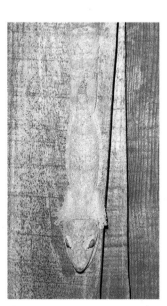

◄ **WOODEN PERFORMANCE** ►
Chameleons are not the only lizards capable of changing their pattern. The Malagasy flat-tailed gecko is also able to alter its appearance, as here to match the wooden planks of a hut (left) and the bark of a tree (right). By combining camouflage with a flattened body edged with thin fringes of skin, this nocturnal gecko can sleep unseen during the day. Its gripping toes mean that it can merge into the background on vertical surfaces or even the undersides of branches. At night it wakes up again to feed.

▲ LEGS LIKE STICKS

The Sri Lankan kangaroo lizard has legs that resemble fine twigs and a body and head patterned to look like a dead leaf or fern frond. When approached by a predator, the kangaroo lizard skips quickly across the forest floor and then disappears into the dead leaves. Often found near forest streams, it can also run across water.

Omen of Evil

Chameleons are considered evil omens in Africa but nowhere are they feared as much as on the island of Madagascar, where the giant panther chameleon is avoided at all costs. Drivers who would not think

twice about hitting a dog or a chicken swerve to avoid chameleons, preferring to risk a serious accident rather than incur the wrath of an angry spirit. Chameleons are also believed by some Malagasy people to be poisonous, so are never handled or eaten even when other meat is scarce.

◀ SPOTLIT SIDES

In 1938 a British naturalist captured a small, cave-dwelling lizard in Trinidad and reported that it had white spots on its flanks that glowed like a ship's portholes. Recently a male lizard was caught and the 1938 report shown to be true. The purpose of the spots is not known but it is thought they might be used to startle predators.

STANDING OUT ▶

Four-fingered skinks are usually brown and blend in with the leaf-litter, but this individual is an albino. Being born an albino can make life more dangerous. Albinos stand out from their surroundings, making them easy targets for predators. Not only are they more likely to be eaten, they are also thought to be vulnerable to sunburn.

Focus on

The beaded lizard and the Gila monster are the world's only venomous lizards. They are found from south-western USA through western Mexico to Guatemala in Central America. Both feed on eggs, fledgling birds and newborn rodents. Since they do not need venom to deal with such harmless prey, it is thought the lizards' poison is mainly to defend against predators. They hang on when they bite, forcing more venom into the wound. Their poison causes great pain, but there are no records of people being killed by these lizards.

RIVER MONSTER
Named after the Gila River, where it was first encountered by settlers, the Gila monster is a spectacular lizard. Its rounded head is covered in large, stud-like scales a little larger than those on its body. Bulges in the rear of the powerful lower jaw indicate the position of the bulbous venom glands.

NO RELATION
It was once thought the Gila monster and beaded lizard might be related to snakes. But the snake has its venom glands and fangs in the upper jaw, while the lizard's venom teeth are in the lower jaw of its skull. This means venom has evolved in these lizards separately from its evolution in snakes.

BEADED BEAST
When seen close up, the beaded lizard is easily distinguished from its northern relative. It isn't as bright as the Gila monster, and its yellow and brown skin camouflage it well. Its head is longer and more squarish, and the neck is longer. The beaded lizard, so called because of its bead-like scales, is larger but less aggressive than the Gila monster.

180

Venomous Lizards

VENOMOUS WARNING

When it feels threatened, the Gila monster opens its mouth like a large blue-tongue skink. But the Gila monster has more to back up its threat than most lizards. Its bite is not only painful but can result in a venomous bite bad enough to require urgent medical attention.

DESERT DWELLER

The Gila monster is most at home in saguero cactus desert. Its bright pink and black markings give out a strong message to potential predators, "Mess with me at your own risk." It may look sluggish, but the Gila monster can move remarkably quickly.

WHERE DO THEY LIVE?

Found in south-west USA and north-west Mexico, from Utah to north Sinaloa, the Gila monster spends much of its life underground, hunting in rodent burrows. It is rarely seen except at dusk or after nightfall.

AT HOME IN THE WOODS

The beaded lizard lives in woodland and scrub in Guatemala, west Mexico and south Sonora. With a longer neck, tail and legs than the Gila monster, it can reach almost 1m (3ft). Although it is in the main a ground-dweller, it can climb trees.

181

Watching Lizards

There are many more lizards in the tropics than in other parts of the world, but lizard watching can be carried out anywhere there are lizards. When watching lizards you are likely to see more if you move slowly and quietly, and stop often to look around. Avoid casting a shadow ahead of you and try to wear drab clothes because some lizards have detailed vision. The best time to see lizards in temperate countries is in the early morning when they come out to bask and are slightly less alert. In the tropics you can find lizards everywhere and at all times of day and night. If you really enjoy lizard watching you might like to go to university and become an herpetologist (a scientist who studies reptiles).

▲ CAUGHT ON CAMERA
Photography is a very satisfying way to record the lizards you find, although not all lizards are as large and impressive as this Komodo dragon, which the author is photographing. A macro lens and a flash gun help capture all the detail in small lizards.

▲ QUIET CONTEMPLATION
Observations from a short distance away must be made without disturbing the lizards. Approach very quietly and slowly and avoid casting your shadow across them, like this herpetologist who is watching sand lizards in Dorset, England.

KEEPING WATCH ▶
Lizards are very common in the tropics and they can be found in many places. These two herpetologists are searching for green-blooded skinks high on Mount Wilhelm, the tallest mountain in Papua New Guinea. Binoculars help you scan branches for small species but you will still have to look very hard and be able to identify what you are looking at when you find it.

SPOTTERS' GUIDE ▶

Lizards include many
different families and
a lizard watcher
must learn how to
identify them. A
knowledge of head
shape, size of scales
and so on is often helpful.
Closely related species may look
very similar, but looking at markings or
counting the number of the scales on the head
helps make an accurate identification.

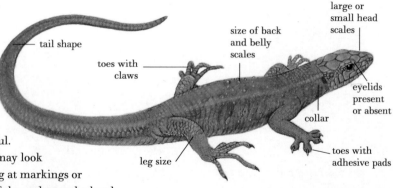

tail shape

size of back
and belly
scales

large or
small head
scales

toes with
claws

eyelids
present
or absent

collar

toes with
adhesive pads

leg size

*This drawing shows features
from several lizards*

◀ IN THE FIELD

The ultimate lizard watching must be carrying out
fieldwork in the tropics. Working in a reserve
studying all the lizards found there is very satisfying.
This sort of fieldwork requires a good background
knowledge and equipment such as a microscope to
examine scales in order to identify species.
Herpetologists often discover new species when
working in remote parts of the world.

▼ HOW TO HOLD LIZARDS

When holding lizards it is important to
support them so that they cannot fall or
injure themselves trying to escape. Lizards
can bite and scratch. This young green
iguana is being held so that it cannot bite
and its legs are secured beside its body. You
should never grab a lizard by its tail.

Great Gecko
*There is just one Delcourt's
giant gecko at the Natural
History Museum in
Marseilles in France.
Collected some time
between 1833 and 1869, it
went unnoticed until 1979
when experts examined it
and found it was a new
species. More than 60cm
(2ft) long, it is twice the
size of any other gecko. No
one is sure where it came
from, but it may have
come from New Zealand.*

Human Threats

Wild lizards are threatened by humans in many varied ways. People collect and kill them for their meat, their skins, their eggs and their internal organs. They are also caught to be sold as pets, particularly the rarer and more exotic species. Many lizards are killed out of fear — chameleons and geckos are considered devils by some native peoples, for example. Many lizards die simply because they make the mistake of looking for insects on a busy road. Less obvious threats include habitat destruction and the introduction of new predators, such as cats or rats. Island lizard species are particularly vulnerable to introduced predators since they usually have only small populations and may be found nowhere else. Other introduced animals, such as goats, may destroy lizards' habitats, leaving them with nowhere to live.

▲ KILLED FOR FASHION
This monitor lizard skin was found by Mark O'Shea when he joined a police raid on one of the large illegal factories in Asia in which wild reptiles are killed and skinned in huge numbers. Lizard-skin handbags, shoes, belts and coats are still popular fashion items. The police found sacks of skins from monitor lizards and pythons, and they rescued and released live reptiles.

◀ CAUGHT FOR THE POT
Tribal rainforest people have always eaten reptiles and other animals. Such small-scale hunting does no real damage but when hunters start supplying markets in the towns it becomes a serious problem. These green iguanas are alive but in shock. Keeping them alive means that their meat stays fresh for the customer.

▲ HABITAT DESTRUCTION

Tropical rainforests have been shrinking for many years due to 'slash and burn' farming and clearance of trees for timber. The result is massive loss of habitat and the disappearance of many forest species.

▲ GORY SOUVENIRS

Although endangered species are protected by international laws, in some countries they can still be found for sale to tourists. This shop is selling stuffed monitor lizards, pythons and cobras, reptiles that are all becoming very rare in the wild. Buying this type of souvenir may lead to the buyer being prosecuted when they return to their own country.

▼ TERRIBLE CONSEQUENCES

Introducing destructive animals to a new place can have catastrophic results. When the brown tree snake was introduced to the island of Guam, it began eating the native geckos, skinks and flightless birds. Now the lizards are very rare and most of the flightless birds have become extinct.

▲ DANGER ON THE ROAD

Lizards cross roads to hunt, find mates or move to new areas. Many, such as this Namibian flapneck chameleon, are too slow to get out of the way of cars. The death toll in some areas is huge. Near many busy towns, wildlife has been almost wiped out.

185

▲ LOOKING AFTER THE LAND
There is no point protecting a species if the habitat in which it lives is not also protected. Unique habitats such as this heathland often contain species found nowhere else. If the habitat is threatened the species may become extinct. Many habitats are destroyed and their species lost before anything has been done to save them.

▲ PROTECTIVE PENS
Conservation usually involves fieldwork. Biologists on Komodo are monitoring the hatching of baby Komodo dragons. They must catch all the hatchlings soon after they emerge from the nest. The metal screening around the nest protects the dragons.

Conservation

Individual species can be protected and so can habitats. Conservation means all the ways there are of protecting and looking after wildlife for the future. Breeding endangered species in captivity is an important part of conservation as is education of people in places where animals are threatened. The education of young people is very important because one day they will be the decision-makers with the power to decide what happens to threatened species. Conservation also involves fighting against illegal trade and the smuggling of animal skins, meat and live reptiles for the pet trade.

▼ CAPTIVE BREEDING
One way to help endangered species is to breed them in captivity. The monkey-tail skink was threatened in its native Solomon Islands, so zoos in the USA and Europe began breeding them in captivity. Researchers have learnt a lot about these lizards and the way the nurturing females behave. Populations built up in projects like this can be used to provide animals for reintroduction into the wild in the future.

EDUCATING PEOPLE ►

Education is an important part of conservation. If people do not know about animals they are less likely to care if they become extinct. Education helps people to see how interesting their local wildlife is. This wildlife park in the New Forest tells people about British reptiles. Wildlife can also be valuable — Komodo islanders earn their livings from tourists who come to see the dragons.

◄ KEEPING TRACK

Baby Komodo dragons have been captured and are being weighed inside a little cage. A few of them will be fitted with radio-tracking devices so that researchers can follow their daily activity in the forest once they have been released. The dragons spend the first two years of life in the trees and without transmitters it would be impossible to find them, let alone follow them.

Did you know? The sand lizard is Britain's rarest lizard. Destruction of habitat threatens its survival!

DRIFT FENCE ►

Many lizards live in leaf-litter and the top layers of soil. Drift fences are used to capture burrowing lizards. They come to the surface at night after rain and bump into the fence. They travel along it and fall into buckets buried along its length. By looking at what ends up in the buckets, scientists can find out which species live on the forest floor.

187

TURTLES

The most ancient reptiles are the turtles,
tortoises and terrapins, known collectively
as chelonians. They have lived on the
Earth since the time of the dinosaurs.
Their generally slow, plodding movement
and distinctive shell make them easier to
see and recognize than many other reptiles.
Yet much of their lives remain mysterious,
especially the extensive wanderings of sea
turtles through the oceans. The huge
variety of chelonians ranges from softshells,
snapping turtles and the pig-nosed turtle
to stinkpot turtles, the spider tortoise
and giant tortoises, which can live for
hundreds of years.

What Are Turtles and Tortoises?

Turtles, tortoises and terrapins make up a group of reptiles called chelonians. They have lived on the Earth for more than 220 million years, since the days of the earliest dinosaurs.

There are about 300 different kinds of chelonian, living in warm places all over the world. Those types that live in the sea are called turtles. Other types of chelonian have different names in different countries. In the UK, for example, those that live on land are tortoises, and those that live in fresh water are called terrapins. In the USA, however, most freshwater chelonians are called turtles, while in Australia they are called tortoises.

▲ OCEAN FLYERS

The green sea turtle is the largest of the sea turtles with hard shells. There are seven types of sea turtle, and they all have flattened, streamlined shells and powerful front flippers. They 'fly' gracefully through the water but move clumsily on land, and cannot pull their head and neck back into the shell as many land chelonians can.

STAR TURN ▼

With its high, domed shell, this Indian star tortoise looks like a walking tank. Only the head, legs and tail stick out of the shell, which has a top and a bottom part and goes right around the body. The stumpy legs are strong, like an elephant's, to support its weight. Land chelonians usually have these pillar-like legs. Those that live in water usually have webbed toes or flippers.

upper shell, or carapace, provides protection from predators

large scales, called scutes, cover the bone of the shell

flexible neck muscles and loose skin allow the tortoise to pull its whole neck inside its shell at times of danger

scaly skin helps prevent the tortoise from drying out

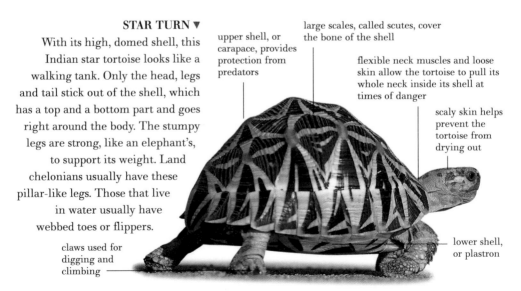

claws used for digging and climbing

lower shell, or plastron

Turtle Who Taught Us

In the children's book Alice's Adventures in Wonderland, *by Lewis Carroll, Alice meets a character called the Mock Turtle, who is often upset and cries easily. He tells Alice a story about his school days, when he had an old turtle as a teacher. Alice is puzzled as to why the old turtle was called Tortoise. The Mock Turtle explains that the teacher was called Tortoise because he 'taught us'.*

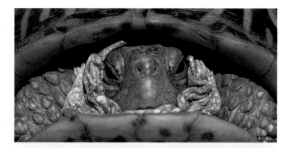

▲ STRAIGHT BACK OR SIDES

Chelonians are divided into two groups according to the way they tuck their head inside their shell. Some fold the neck straight back on itself in a tight S-shape (top). The others bend their neck sideways under the lip of the top shell, leaving the neck and head slightly exposed at the front (bottom).

▼ TASTY TERRAPIN

The diamond-backed terrapin lives in the shallow marshes along North America's Atlantic coast, where fresh water and salt water mix together. For a hundred years or so, this terrapin was hunted for its tasty meat. Much of its habitat was also destroyed, and the terrapin almost became extinct. Today, thanks to conservation and changes in eating habits, numbers are recovering.

▲ BRAVE NEW WORLD

All chelonians lay shelled eggs on land, even those that live in the sea. This is because the young need to breathe oxygen from the air. When the baby chelonian is ready to hatch, it uses an egg tooth on its snout to cut through the shell. The egg tooth is a hard scale, not a real tooth. Even with the help of the egg tooth, escaping from the shell is a slow process.

191

Familiar Faces

There are hundreds of different kinds, or species, of chelonian. These are grouped into twelve families, based on the features that they have in common. The biggest of these families has about 90 species, but four families contain only one species because there are no other chelonians that are quite like them. Chelonians such as land tortoises and sea turtles may be quite familiar to you. The largest and smallest chelonians belong to these families. The largest is the leatherback sea turtle, which tips the scales at 680kg (1,500lb) or more, while the tiny speckled padloper tortoise weighs less than 220g (9oz) and would easily fit on your hand.

▲ LAND TORTOISES

Land tortoises, such as this leopard tortoise, belong to the family Testudinidae. This is the second largest family, with more than 50 species, living mainly in hot areas of Africa, India, South-east Asia and South America. A few species live in cooler areas of southern Europe, western Asia and southern North America. The land tortoise family includes the giant tortoises of the Galapagos Islands and Aldabra. Land tortoises generally have a domed, bony shell and strong, stocky legs equipped with claws for digging. They eat mainly plants.

SEA TURTLES ▶

Six species of hard-shelled sea turtle belong to the Cheloniidae family. These are the hawksbill (right), green, flatback, loggerhead, Kemp's Ridley and olive Ridley turtles. The giant leatherback turtle, with its soft, leathery shell, is so unusual that it is placed in a separate family. Sea turtles spend most of their lives in the ocean, but females lay their eggs on land. Their legs are shaped like flippers, and they cannot pull their head and neck back inside their shell.

POND TURTLES ▶

This slider, or red-eared terrapin, belongs to the largest and most varied group of chelonians, the Emydidae. There are more than 90 species in this family of pond turtles, members of which live on all continents except Australia and Antarctica. The top shell is shaped like a low arch, and some species have a movable hinge in the bottom shell. The legs of pond turtles are developed for swimming, and some are slightly webbed between the toes.

◀ POND TURTLE GROUPS

The pond turtle family, the Emydidae, is divided into two smaller subfamilies. The Batagurinae live in Europe, Africa and Asia. The Indian black turtle (left) belongs to this group, as does the spiny turtle, the Asian leaf turtle and the European pond turtle. The other group, the Emydinae, lives in parts of North, Central and South America. It includes species such as the slider, the spotted turtle, the wood turtle, the ornate box turtle and the painted turtle.

MUD OR MUSK TURTLES ▼

Members of the mud or musk turtle family, including the loggerhead musk turtle (below), live in an area ranging from Canada to South America. These small chelonians are named after the musky-smelling substances they produce when they are disturbed. These strong smells drive away any enemies. These turtles live in fresh water and one of their special characteristics is webs between their toes. Their legs are specially adapted for crawling along the muddy bottom of marshes, swamps and rivers. The bottom shell may have one or two movable hinges.

Did you know? The green turtle is named after its green body fat.

Strange Species

Did you know that there is a turtle with a face like a pig? This is just one of the many strange and surprising species of chelonians. They include the formidable snapping turtles and unusual softshells, and a turtle with a head too big for its own shell. There are also the strange side-necked turtles, which bend their neck sideways under their shell. Side-necked turtles were more common in the past, and one extinct species may have been the largest freshwater turtle that ever lived. It grew to a length of 230cm (90in), which is twice as long as the largest side-necked turtle alive today – the Arrau river turtle.

▲ SNAPPING TURTLES

The two types of the North American snapping turtle are the only chelonians that can be dangerous to people. They are named after their powerful, snapping jaws, and have terrible tempers when provoked, which makes them very hard to handle. The bottom shell of snapping turtles is small and shaped like a cross, which makes it easier for them to move their legs in muddy water and among thick water plants.

Did you know? Pig-nosed turtles in Australia have been known to eat giant fruit bats.

▼ SOFTSHELL TURTLES

The 22 species of softshell turtle have a flattened top shell covered with a leathery skin instead of a hard, horny covering. Their aggressive nature makes up to some extent for the poor protection given by their softer shells. Softshell turtles are agile, expert swimmers, with legs like paddles. The tip of their nose is a long tube with the nostrils at the very end. This means they can stay under water and breathe by just pushing their nostrils above the water's surface. Softshell turtles live in Africa, Asia and North America.

◄ BIG-HEADED TURTLE

The unique big-headed turtle is the only member of its family, Platysternidae. Its huge head is almost half the width of its top shell, far too big to be drawn back inside the shell. The skull has a solid bony roof for protection, and the head is covered by an extra-tough horny layer. Living in cool mountain streams in South-east Asia, the big-headed turtle comes out at night to catch small fish and other water creatures in its hooked jaws.

PIG-NOSED TURTLE ▼

The weird pig-nosed turtle has a snout that sticks out, like softshell turtles, but its nose is shorter, wrinkled and has the nostrils at the side, making it look like a pig. Another extraordinary feature is its front legs, which look like the flippers of sea turtles. The pig-nosed turtle lives in the rivers and lakes of Papua New Guinea and northern Australia. One river it inhabits is called the Fly River, so it is also named the Fly River turtle. It is the only member of the Carettochelyidae family.

◄ SIDE-NECKED TURTLES

There are about 60 species of side-necked turtles, such the yellow-spotted Amazon River turtle (left). Some of them have such long necks that they are called snake-necked turtles. Side-necked turtles are divided into two groups. One group, Pelomedusidae, lives only in South America, Africa and on some of the Indian Ocean islands. The other group, Chelidae, inhabits South America and the Australian region. They all live in freshwater habitats, such as streams, rivers, lakes and swamps, and their back feet are strongly webbed for swimming.

Focus on

The world's largest tortoises all live on islands – the Galapagos Islands in the Pacific Ocean and the coral atoll of Aldabra in the Indian Ocean. The Galapagos tortoises are up to 130cm (50in) long, and they can weigh 275kg (605lb) – that is as heavy as three men. It is likely that these giant tortoises reached the islands by floating over the ocean on rafts of plants or debris. The Aldabra tortoise probably came from Madagascar, while the Galapagos tortoises came from the mainland of South America.

SWIMMING LESSONS

Aldabra tortoises sometimes swim out to sea. This one is just climbing up the beach after swimming. In the water, the tortoise bobs up and down among the waves like a cork but does not swim very well.

SHELL SHAPES

Twelve species of giant tortoise live on the Galapagos Islands. These probably all evolved from a common ancestor, but each species then adapted to the different conditions on the different islands. For example, the shells of each species have a certain shape and thickness according to the habitat in which they live. Tortoises that live on the large and wet islands have thick, domed shells. On the smaller islands, which are drier and have fewer plants growing on them, the giant tortoises have long necks and legs and a shell that turns upwards behind the neck like a horse's saddle. This 'saddleback' shell (left) allows the tortoises to stretch their necks upwards to feed on taller plants, so they can collect enough food. The word *galapagos* is an old Spanish word for a kind of saddle that is turned up at the front, like the shells of the saddleback tortoises.

Island Giants

LITTLE AND LARGE
This Aldabra tortoise looks absolutely vast next to the world's smallest tortoise, a speckled padloper (roadwalker), or Cape tortoise. The speckled padloper has a shell as small as 10cm (4in) long, whereas the Aldabra tortoise has a shell up to 105cm (40in) long and weighs as much as 120kg (265lb).

TORTOISE COMPETITION
During the breeding season, male Galapagos tortoises are noisy while they are courting females, making loud roaring noises. They are also aggressive towards other males, charging and butting them with their heads. Saddleback males even have neck-stretching contests, to see which of them can reach the highest.

BATH-TIME
These giant Galapagos tortoises are soaking themselves in a muddy pool. This helps them to cool down, because large tortoises cannot lose heat as efficiently as smaller ones. Compared with the large volume of their bodies, the giants have a relatively small surface area through which their body heat can escape. Soaking in pools may also help the tortoises to get rid of ticks, mites and other parasites living on the outside of their bodies.

TURTLES

The Turtle Shell

No other animal has body protection quite like a chelonian's shell. The shell shields the animal from the weather and also from predators, and it will regrow if it is damaged. It also supports soft muscles and organs, such as the heart and lungs, inside the body. The shell is made of bony plates, which are covered by giant scales called scutes. Land chelonians typically have high-domed or knobbly shells to protect them from predators. Water chelonians have lighter, streamlined shells.

▲ TOPS AND BOTTOMS
Every turtle shell has a top part, known as the carapace, and a bottom part, the plastron. You can clearly see these on this upside-down Florida box turtle. The two parts of the shell are locked together on each side by bony bridges.

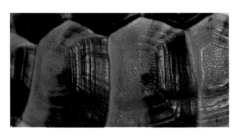

◄ HOW OLD?
Many chelonians have growth rings on their scutes. The rings represent a period of slow growth, such as during a dry season. It is not a very reliable method, however, to work out the age of a chelonian by counting the rings, because more than one ring may form in a year, and some rings may be worn away.

SOFTSHELLS ►
Named after their soft, leathery shells, softshell turtles also have a bony shell underneath. The bones have air spaces in them, which help the turtle float in water. Their flat shells make it easier for softshells to hide in soft mud and sand as they lie in wait for their prey.

▲ FLAT AS A PANCAKE

The shell of the African pancake tortoise lives up to its name, being much flatter than those of other land species. This allows the tortoise to squeeze into narrow crevices under rocks to avoid predators and the hot sun. The flexible carapace also helps with this, and the tortoises use their legs and claws to fix themselves firmly in position. Once the tortoise has wedged itself in between the rocks, it is extremely difficult to remove it.

▲ SHELL PROBLEMS

This young marginated tortoise has a deformed shell because it has been fed on the wrong food. Pet chelonians should be given mineral and vitamin supplements as well as the correct food in order to keep them healthy.

▲ TURTLE IN A BOX

Some chelonians, such as this box turtle, have a hinge on the plastron. This allows them to pull the head, legs and tail inside and shut the shell completely. In some species, this gives protection from predators, but protection against loss of moisture may also be important. African hinge-back tortoises have a hinge on the carapace rather than on the plastron.

Turtle World
Turtle shells are very strong. The strongest ones can support a weight over 200 times heavier than the body of the turtle – that's like you having nine cars on your back! According to Hindu beliefs, the Earth is supported by four elephants standing on the back of a turtle that is floating in the Universal Ocean.

How the Body Works

Chelonians have a skeleton both inside and outside their bodies. There is the bony shell on the outside, and on the inside there is a bony skeleton made up of the skull, backbone and ribs, and the leg, hip and shoulder bones.

Just like humans, chelonians use oxygen from the air to work their muscles, and this gets into the blood through the lungs. When we breathe in, our chest moves out to draw air into our lungs, but chelonians' ribs are fused to their shell, so they cannot expand their chest in this way. Instead, they use muscles between the front legs to force air in and out of the body.

scute

spine bones

carapace

plastron

▲ SPECIAL SKELETON

The shell of a chelonian is its outside skeleton, while inside the body is a framework of bones that provides an anchor for the muscles and protects the delicate internal organs. Apart from in the leatherback turtle, the spine bones and ribs are fused to the carapace (the top part of the shell).

SWIMMING BONES ▼

The most obvious features of a sea turtle's skeleton are the extremely long toe bones that support the front flippers. The toe bones of the back feet are also long and slim. Chelonians have eight neck bones (mammals have seven) and between 40 and 50 bones in their backbone (you have 33 of these bones). You can see how the shoulder and hip bones fit inside the ribs so the shell can cover the whole body. Most other animals have their shoulder and hip bones outside their ribs.

hip bones

shoulder bones

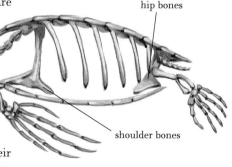

WINDOW ON THE BODY ▶

If you could see inside a chelonian's body, you would be able to see its heart, lungs and other internal organs. A three-chambered heart pumps the blood around the body. (Most reptiles have hearts with three chambers, while mammals, have four heart chambers.) The digestive system works fairly slowly, and food takes days to pass through the body. The digestive, excretory and reproductive systems all end in one chamber called the cloaca.

The hole where the cloaca opens to the outside may be called the cloaca, anus or vent.

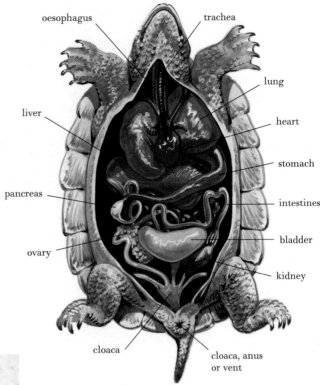

oesophagus
trachea
liver
lung
heart
stomach
pancreas
intestines
ovary
bladder
kidney
cloaca
cloaca, anus or vent

◀ TURTLE TAILS

Chelonian tails come in a variety of lengths and thicknesses, and are particularly long in snapping turtles. The big-headed turtle also has a long tail, which it uses as a brace to help it climb. Male chelonians (shown here on the left) often have longer and heavier tails than females (on the right), which usually have short, stubby tails. This is one way of telling the sexes apart.

SNORKEL NOSE ▶

Some freshwater chelonians, such as this snake-necked turtle, have a long neck and a tube-like nose that works like a snorkel. They can stay under water and just push their nostrils up above the surface to breathe air. As well as breathing air into their lungs, some freshwater chelonians also extract oxygen from the water. The oxygen is absorbed through areas of thin skin inside the throat and rear opening, or cloaca.

Temperature Check

Chelonians are cold-blooded. This does not mean that chelonians are cold. They need heat to keep their bodies working properly, but they cannot produce this heat themselves as mammals and birds do. Instead, their body temperature rises and falls with that of their surroundings. They control body temperature by basking in the sun to warm up and moving into the shade or water to cool down. In places with very cold or very hot seasons, chelonians may take shelter and go into a long sleep.

▼ SUNBATHING

On sunny days chelonians, such as these side-necked turtles, often bask in the sun to warm up. The extra warmth from the sunlight can speed up digestion and may help turtles to make Vitamin D, needed for healthy bones and shells. Females bask more than males because they need extra warmth for making eggs.

▲ CHILLY SWIMMER

The leatherback sea turtle swims farther into the cold northern and southern oceans than any other sea turtle. It has special ways of keeping warm in the cold water. Its dark body probably helps it to absorb the Sun's heat. The leatherback's muscles also produce heat, and this is trapped in the body by its thick, oily skin, which has a layer of fat underneath it. These turtles also have an ingenious system that keeps their flippers colder than the rest of the body, so heat is not lost as the turtle swims.

SUN SHELTER ▶

In hot climates, many land tortoises, such as this Mediterranean tortoise, need to shelter from the heat of the Sun. They seek out the shade cast by bushes or trees, or retreat into underground burrows. The tortoises dig out the burrows with their front legs, often making large chambers for resting or sleeping. Sometimes they sleep in their burrow throughout a hot season – this is called aestivation. The cool, moist tortoise burrows may also provide a refuge for other animals, such as mice, frogs and lizards.

◀ HOW TO HIBERNATE

Tortoises that sleep throughout the cold season in the wild also need to do so when in captivity. This deep winter sleep is called hibernation. Before hibernating your pet tortoise, make sure it is fit, has enough body fat and that there is no food in its gut. During hibernation, the tortoise must be dry and neither too hot nor too cold. To find out more, contact an organization such as the Tortoise Trust.

DRYING IN THE SUN ▶

A basking yellow-bellied turtle stretches its neck and legs and spreads its toes wide to soak up as much sunshine as possible. Basking makes a turtle drier as well as warmer. This may help it to get rid of algae and parasites growing on its shell. A thick covering of algae would slow the turtle's movement through the water, and it could also damage the shell.

203

Plodders and Swimmers

From slow, plodding land tortoises
to graceful, swimming sea turtles,
chelonians have developed a variety
of types of legs and feet to suit their
surroundings. On land, the heavy shell
makes running impossible. It takes a
land tortoise about five hours to walk
just 1.6km (1 mile)! Sea turtles, with
their powerful flippers, can reach the
greatest swimming speeds of any
living reptile. Some swim as fast as
30kph (20mph), which is as fast as
humans can run on land. Freshwater
chelonians have webbed feet for speed
in swimming. Some chelonians make
regular migration journeys to find
food or nesting places.

▲ ELEPHANT LEGS
Land chelonians, such as this giant tortoise,
have back legs like sturdy columns, which
help to support them. The front legs may be
like clubs or flattened and more like shovels,
which helps with digging.

◄ FLIPPER FEET
The strong, flat flippers of
sea turtles have no toes on
the outside, although inside
the flippers are five long toe
bones bound together into
one stiff unit. The front
flippers are used to propel
the turtle through the water,
while the back ones act as
rudders and brakes. There
are only one or two claws on
each flipper, and leatherback
turtles have no claws at all.
This makes the flippers
more streamlined.

◄ **SEASONAL WALKABOUT**
Some freshwater chelonians, such as the spotted turtle (left) and wood turtle of North America, migrate on to land in the summer for feeding and nesting. In winter they return to swamps, pools and rivers to hibernate during the cold weather. On these short migrations, the turtles often have to cross roads. They run the risk of being run over, especially as they move so slowly.

WEBBED TOES ►
The feet of freshwater turtles have long toes joined together by webs, creating a bigger surface area to push against the water. They use all four legs to paddle along, but the back ones provide most of the pushing power. Freshwater chelonians also have gripping claws for walking on land and on the bottom of ponds and streams.

▲ FRESHWATER FLIPPERS
The pig-nosed turtle is the only freshwater turtle with flippers. Like a sea turtle, it flies through the water, moving both front flippers at the same time. Other freshwater turtles mainly use their back legs to swim, and move their front legs alternately. The pig-nosed turtle has two claws on the edge of each paddle-like leg. The back claws are used for digging nests.

Slow and Steady Winner
In Aesop's fable The Hare and the Tortoise *a speedy hare boasted about how fast he could run. He made fun of the tortoise, with his short feet and slow walk. But the tortoise just laughed and challenged the hare to a race. The hare thought there was no need to hurry because the tortoise was so slow. Instead of racing, he took a nap by the side of the road. The tortoise just kept plodding slowly along. As the tortoise approached the finish, the loud cheering woke up the hare, but he was too late to win the race.*

Eyes, Ears and Noses

A chelonian's most important senses are sight, taste and smell. The shell and skin are also sensitive to touch. Chelonians probably do not hear very well, although they can pick up vibrations through an ear inside the head. They do not have an ear opening on the outside of the head, as we do. Their eyesight is best at close-range, and they can see details. Good eyesight is useful for finding food, avoiding predators and navigating on long journeys. As well as smelling through their noses, chelonians have a structure in the mouth called the Jacobson's organ. This allows them to detect tiny chemical particles in the air.

▲ VIBRATION DETECTORS
The extraordinary matamata lives in murky waters where it is hard to see clearly. Its eyes are very small, and it does not seem to detect its prey by sight. Instead, it relies on the flaps of skin on its head, which have lots of nerve endings and are very sensitive to vibrations in the water. The flaps pick up signs of prey as the matamata moves through the water, and this helps it to get ready to attack.

Did you know? A chelonian can feel pressure on its shell just as you can on your fingernails.

◄ ON THE CHIN
Many freshwater turtles, such as this side-neck turtle, have fingers of skin, called barbels, dangling under their chins. Snapping turtles have four pairs. Scientists are not sure exactly what the barbels are for, but they seem to be sensory structures. Some Australian side-necks touch each other's barbels during their courtship display.

Robot Turtle

These girls are joining the electrical leads to a robot called a Turtle. Schoolchildren are able to instruct the Turtle robot to make simple movements and draw lines and patterns across a large sheet of paper. Inside the Turtle's see-through shell are the wheels it uses to move about. Working with the Turtle robot helps children learn how computers work and how to give them simple instructions.

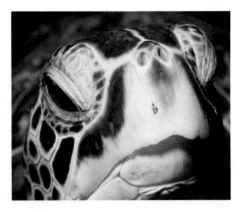

▲ THE EYES HAVE IT

Sea turtles have good vision under the water but are short-sighted on land. Their large upper eyelids protect the eyes while they are swimming. Chelonians also have a third eyelid, called a nictitating membrane. This cleans the eye and keeps it moist, protecting it like a pair of goggles.

▼ TASTY TONGUE

A chelonian's tongue is broad and flat and firmly attached to the bottom of the mouth, which stops it from moving around. Taste buds on the tongue and in the throat are used for tasting food, although the sense of taste is also linked to the sense of smell. This leopard tortoise comes from Africa, and in the wild it eats grasses, prickly pear cacti and thistles.

▼ MR RED-EYE

Adult male box turtles often have red eyes, while the eyes of the females are yellow or brown. A few females also have red eyes, but they are less bright than the males'. Scientists have shown that turtles seem to prefer shades of orange and blue. Japanese turtles can even be trained to tell the difference between red and blue.

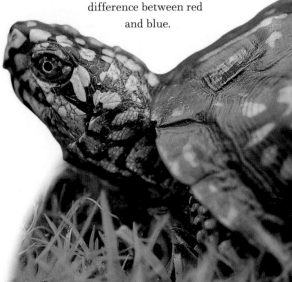

What Chelonians Eat

Chelonians may be herbivores (plant-eaters) or carnivores (meat-eaters), but many of them are omnivores, which means they eat all kinds of food. Some herbivores, such as the cooters of North and Central America, have jaws with jagged edges. This helps them to crush plant food, such as stems and fruits.

The diet of omnivores often changes with age. Young ones tend to eat more insects, while adults either eat more plants or have a more specialized diet. Many chelonians pick up extra nutrients by feeding on dung or dead animals. Also, after eggs have hatched, female offspring may eat the eggshells to help them build a store of calcium for producing the shells of their own eggs.

▲ GRASS FOR LUNCH
A giant Galapagos tortoise uses its horny jaws to bite off pieces of grass. Galapagos tortoises also eat other plants, such as cacti and other fleshy, water-filled plants. In the dry season, these tortoises have to get all their water from their plant food.

NOT A FUSSY EATER ▶
The hawksbill sea turtle is an omnivore that seems to prefer invertebrates (animals without backbones) such as coral, sponges, jellyfish, sea urchins, shrimp and molluscs. Plants in its diet include seaweeds and mangrove fruits, leaves, bark and wood. The hawksbill has a narrow head with jaws meeting at an acute angle. This helps it to reach into narrow cracks in coral reefs and pull out food.

▲ CHANGING DIET

Many chelonians, such as this slider, change their diet as they grow up. Young sliders eat more insects, while adults feed on mainly plants. Some chelonians switch to a whole new diet when they reach adulthood. When males and females are different sizes, they may also have different diets. Female Barbour's map turtles are more than twice the size of the males. They eat mainly shellfish, whereas the males feed mostly on insects.

OPEN WIDE ▶

Chelonians never need to visit the dentist, because they do not have teeth! Instead of teeth, their jaws are lined with hard keratin – the material fingernails are made of. The keratin is either sharpened into cutting edges or broadened into crushing plates. Cutting edges slice through animal bodies, while plates are used to grind plant food. Some ancient turtles had a set of teeth on the roof of their mouth, but did not have proper ones along the edges of the jaws, like most reptiles and other vertebrates.

Feeding Pets

Feeding pet tortoises or turtles is not as simple as you might think. An incorrect diet can lead to growth problems such as soft or deformed shells, and eggs with thin walls that break during laying. It is best to find out what your pet eats in the wild and try to feed it a similar, and varied, diet. Land chelonians eat mostly plants, while those that live in water have more animal food in their diets. High-fat foods, such as cheese, will make your pet overweight, and this is not good for its health. Ask the advice of an organization such as the Tortoise Trust for more information. Most pet chelonians need extra vitamins and minerals to make up for those missing in the prepared foods available from retailers. Water is important, too. Without enough to drink, your pet chelonian may suffer from kidney problems.

Turtle Hunters

Some chelonians have developed special hunting methods, such as lying in wait to ambush their prey or luring their prey towards them. Ambush hunters are usually well camouflaged and have long, muscular necks that can shoot out to grab a meal. Some turtles hide by flipping sand over their bodies or by burying themselves in soft mud. Most chelonians that live in water capture prey by opening their mouth wide and sucking in food and water.

The alligator snapping turtle lures its prey with a worm-like structure on its tongue. Common snapping turtles are more active hunters, grabbing small water birds. Other hunters herd fish into shallow water to make them easier to catch.

▲ SNAKE STRIKE
The common snake-necked turtle is named after its very long neck, which looks a little like a snake. The neck is more than two-thirds the length of the shell, which measures up to 28cm (11in) long. The snake-necked turtle creeps up on its prey and then lunges forward with its long neck, grabbing small creatures such as fish, frogs and worms, before they have time to escape.

BEWARE – AMBUSH! ▶
The spiny softshell turtle often buries itself in mud or sand with only its long head and neck showing. When small animals pass close by, the spiny softshell quickly shoots out its neck and gulps down its meal. To grab large prey, it may almost leap out of its hiding place, showering sand or mud everywhere. Spiny softshells feed on smaller water creatures, such as worms.

▲ WORM DANCE

The wood turtle's omnivorous diet includes earthworms, which come to the surface of the ground after rain. Some wood turtle populations draw earthworms to the surface by stomping their feet to imitate the rain falling on the ground. A stomping turtle stomps with one foot and then the other at a rate of about one stomp per second for about 15 minutes or more. The loudest stomps can be heard 3m (10ft) away.

▲ SLOW FOOD

Few chelonians have the speed or agility to catch fast-moving prey. They usually eat slow-moving creatures, such as worms, insect grubs, caterpillars and molluscs. This Natal hinge-back tortoise is eating a millipede, which is not a speedy creature, despite having lots of legs. The long skull of this tortoise, with its sharp, hooked top jaw, helps it to reach out and grab prey.

VACUUM MEALS ▼

The bizarre matamata from South America is a 'gape-and-suck' predator. It lies on the bottom of muddy rivers, moving so little that a thick growth of algae usually forms on its rough shell. It is so well camouflaged that small fish do not see it. When a fish swims close by, the turtle suddenly opens its huge mouth and expands its large throat, sucking the fish inside. All this happens at lightning speed, too fast for a human to see. The matamata then closes its mouth to a slit, flushing out the water but trapping its meal inside.

211

Focus on

Can you imagine savage turtles with bad tempers and jaws strong enough to bite off your fingers? The two kinds of snapping turtles of the Americas are just like this. The alligator snapping turtle is the heaviest freshwater turtle, growing to a length of 66cm (26in) and weighing as much as 80kg (176lb). The common snapping turtle is smaller, but still grows a carapace as long as 47cm (19in). Both kinds of snapping turtle live at the bottom of rivers and lakes. The common snapper is a prowling predator, stalking its prey with a slow-motion walk before grabbing it with a rapid strike. The alligator snapper sometimes hunts like this, but it usually sits with its mouth open and waits for food to swim into its jaws. Both of the snapping turtles are omnivores, eating algae and fruit, as well as lots of animals, from insects and crabs to fish and muskrats.

LURING PREY

The alligator snapping turtle has a red worm-like lure on its tongue. The turtle wriggles this 'worm' so that it looks alive. Hungry fish swim into the huge jaws to investigate the bait. The turtle then swallows small fish whole or pierces larger ones with the hooked tips of its strong jaws.

HANDLE WITH CARE

The common snapping turtle strikes with amazing speed, shooting out its head and biting with its sharp jaws. You can often hear the crunching sound as the jaws snap shut. It should only ever be approached by an expert, who will handle it only if absolutely necessary. When handled, these turtles also give off a musky scent.

Snapping Turtles

CRAFTY CAMOUFLAGE

The alligator snapping turtle is well camouflaged by its muddy-brown shell and skin. The bumps and lumps on its shell also help to break up its outline, so it is hard to see on the bottom of dark, slow-moving rivers. It keeps so still that a thick growth of algae usually grows on its rough shell, making it almost invisible to passing fish.

VARIED MENU

This snapping turtle is eating a young duck, but it is also strong enough to seize larger water birds by the feet and drag them under the water. Snapping turtles have a varied diet, which includes fish, dead animals, small water creatures and a surprising amount of plant material. The stomach of one snapping turtle caught in Columbia, South America, contained the remains of 101 freshwater snails.

BASKING BY DAY

During the day, the snapping turtle often floats beneath the surface of the water, with only its eyes and nostrils above the surface. It may also bask like this to warm up. If it is disturbed, the turtle can react with surprising speed. It is more active by night than during the day.

Courtship

Chelonians usually live on their own and
meet only for mating. Depending on the
environment, mating may occur all year
round or just during agreeable seasons.
The sexes are often difficult to tell apart,
though they may be of different sizes or
have tails of different lengths. Some males
develop brighter markings on their body
during the breeding season. Males seem to
find their mates largely by sight, although
some females, such as musk turtles, release
scents to attract males. Some males bob
their heads up and down or stroke the faces
of females in an attempt to persuade them
to mate. Females may also take part in the
courtship dance.

▲ **FIGHTING FOR FEMALES**
Chelonians are aggressive fighters,
and rival males, such as these desert
tortoises, fight over females. They
push, shove, bite and kick, sometimes
wounding each other, until one gives
up and beats a retreat. Sometimes one
male flips his rival right over on to his
back. It is difficult for upside-down
chelonians to turn the right way up
again. More often, the weaker male
decides to beat a retreat rather than
risk being injured by a stronger rival.

▼ **SIZE DIFFERENCE**
In this picture, which do you think is the male and
which is the female? For many chelonians, the males
and females are almost the same size. However, for
nearly all land-living tortoises, females are larger
than males. The small male leopard tortoise in the
photograph is in fact chasing the larger female. In the
case of giant tortoises and alligator snapping turtles,
however, males are much larger than the females.

COURTSHIP DISPLAY ▼

Before chelonians mate, they may take part in a courtship dance. A male gopher tortoise, for example, bobs his head up and down and circles around the female. He bites her shell and legs (right) and crashes into her to try to force her to stand still for mating.

▼ MATING TIME

During mating, the male climbs on top of the carapace of the female. Males of many species have a hollow in the bottom of their shell, which fits around the female's shell. The male uses its claws to grip the female's shell. Many chelonians, such as these giant Galapagos tortoises, bellow and grunt during mating. In this case, the male is larger than the female and finds it difficult to heave himself into a mating position.

▲ CURIOUS CLAWS

Some male turtles, such as painted turtles, have three long claws on their front feet. Courtship begins with the male chasing the female through the water. When he overtakes her, the male turns to face the female and strokes her face with his claws. If the female wants to mate, she strokes the male's legs. The male then attempts to make the female follow him. She will sink to the bottom, where the pair mate.

LOOK AT ME ▶

In the breeding season a few males become much brighter to help them attract females. For example, male wood turtles develop bright orange skin on their neck and front legs. They pose in front of the females to show off their breeding signals, stretching out the neck and turning the head from side to side. Wood turtles also carry out a dance before mating. This involves walking towards each other and swinging their heads from side to side. The dance may go on for as long as two hours.

Eggs and Nests

All chelonians lay eggs on land because their young need to breathe oxygen from the air. Females usually dig a nest in sand, soil or rotting leaves. Apart from one species, the females do not stay to look after their eggs. The size and number of eggs vary enormously from species to species. Female African pancake tortoises lay one egg at a time, and giant Galapagos tortoises lay less than 15 eggs, but many sea turtles produce more than 100 eggs at a time. Several species may lay two or more clutches of eggs in one breeding season. The smallest eggs are less than 2.5cm (1in) in diameter, while the largest measure up to 7.6cm (3in).

▲ SANDY NESTS

Female sea turtles dig nests for their eggs on sandy beaches. Their eggs are soft and flexible, which means there is less danger of them cracking when they are dropped into the nest. Soft shells also use up less calcium and can absorb moisture. Young grow faster in soft shells than those in harder ones, which allows them to escape before beaches are flooded by the sea. Flooding kills the eggs because it cuts off the oxygen supply to the young.

◄ EGG LAYING

This Hermann's tortoise is laying her eggs in a hollow she has dug in the ground. The eggs have to fit through the opening at the back of her shell, so they cannot be too large. Larger females can lay bigger eggs. Many chelonians use their back legs to arrange the eggs as they are laid, sometimes into two or three layers separated by thin partitions of soil.

Did you know? A hawksbill turtle once laid as many as 258 eggs in just one clutch.

▼ GUARD DUTY

The Asian brown, or Burmese, tortoise is the only land species known to defend its nest. The female builds a large nest mound of dead leaves by sweeping the material backwards for up to 4m (13ft) around the nest. After she has laid her eggs, the female guards the nest for up to three days, which helps to protect the eggs from predators.

◄ ROUND EGGS

The red-footed tortoise lays round eggs with hard shells. Eggs with hard shells do not lose water as easily as those with soft shells. The round shape also helps to reduce water-loss because it has the minimum possible ratio of surface area to volume. In other words, there is less surface from which the liquid inside can leak out. Hard-shelled eggs are brittle, however, and are more likely to crack than soft-shelled ones. Giant tortoises produce sticky slime around their eggs to cushion the impact as they fall into a deep nest.

▲ CAPTIVE BREEDING

Many chelonians are bred in captivity. Most of these animals are sold as pets or for food so that they do not need to be taken from the wild. Captive breeding is also a good way of increasing the numbers of rare chelonians. Artificial incubators (above) copy the conditions inside nests, keeping the eggs warm and moist enough for proper development. In the case of chelonians, such as box turtles and most tropical tortoises, the developing embryo will die or be deformed if the eggs dry out too much.

Focus on Green

Green turtles breed for the first time when they are between 25 and 50 years old. When they are ready to mate, both males and females migrate from their feeding grounds to courtship areas close to nesting beaches. Nesting beaches are in warm places around the world, from Central America and the Pacific islands to the shores of Africa and South-east Asia. Some may travel as much as 2,000km (1,245 miles).

Green turtles nest every two or three years. They lay several clutches during a nesting year, about two weeks apart. A female comes ashore in the cool of the night to lay eggs, dragging herself slowly up the beach. After digging a pit with her flippers, she lays her eggs in it. Then she sweeps sand over her eggs and heads back to the sea.

MATING IN WATER

These green turtles are mating in water. Mating in the water is easier than on land because the water supports the weight of the male's body. This means he is not as heavy on top of the female. Males of many sea turtles have hook-like claws on their front flippers to grip the front edges of the female's carapace and help them stay in position while they mate.

DIGGING THE NEST

A female green turtle digs her nest on her own, using her front flippers at first to throw sand out of the way, then her back flippers to scrape out a hole. The nest is as deep as the length of the her back flipper. She lays about 120 eggs, which are the size of ping-pong balls. The whole process takes up to four hours, as many false nests may be dug and abandoned.

Turtle Nests

COVERING THE EGGS

When the female green turtle has finished laying her eggs, she disguises the nest chamber by sweeping sand into the hole. She uses all four flippers to do this, making a mound of sand. After kneading the sand mound for some time, the female throws sand over the spot again to make it hard for predators to find.

BACK TO THE SEA

After the female has hidden the nest as well as she can, she hauls her heavy body back down the beach to the sea, taking regular rests. She will have to crawl a long way because the nest must be far up the beach so that it is on dry sand, out of reach of the high tides.

HATCHING OUT

About two months after they are laid, the eggs hatch. The baby green turtles work together to dig out of the nest. It takes them three days to struggle out. Eventually, on a cool evening, the babies rush down to the sea, hoping to avoid falling prey to predators, such as raccoons.

SWIMMING BABES

Hatchlings that do manage to reach the sea dive into the waves and ride the undertow out to sea. They swim continuously for 24–48 hours until they reach deeper water, where they are less at risk from predators, such as sharks. Only one or two out of the clutch live long enough to breed.

Hatching and Young

▲ BREAKING FREE

The trigger for a baby chelonian to hatch is the need for more oxygen. A hatching turtle makes a hole in its shell using a sharp little scale called an egg tooth, on the tip of its snout. This falls off within a few weeks. As well as pushing at the shell with its egg tooth, the hatchling bites pieces from the shell and pushes with its legs. Escape can be a slow process, taking several hours.

The amount of time it takes for chelonian eggs to hatch varies enormously, but warmer temperatures speed up the process. For many chelonians, the temperature in the nest also determines the sex of the hatchlings. Higher temperatures tend to lead to more females being born. For some species, such as snapping turtles, however, both higher or lower temperatures than average produce more females. Species from cooler climates usually take from two to three months to hatch, whereas tropical species take from four months to over a year. The shortest incubation times are for the Chinese softshell (40–80 days) and the giant South American river turtle (50 days). The chelonian with the longest incubation time is the leopard tortoise of Africa. Its eggs take over a year to hatch.

A QUICK REST ▶

Once a hatching chelonian has opened the shell to allow oxygen to enter, it often stays in the egg for a day or more. This gives it time to grow stronger before escaping from the shell. A yolk sac, which has kept the baby alive during its development, provides a food reserve. You can see the pink yolk sac inside this shell. This is gradually absorbed into the hatchling's body in a few hours or days, giving it extra energy. Then the hatchling is able to move about easily.

▲ ESCAPE TUNNEL

For turtles that hatch in an underground nest, such as these olive Ridley sea turtles, the first thing they have to do is to reach the surface. Hatchling turtles are good at digging, but it may take the efforts of all the hatchlings in a nest to break free into the open air.

▲ FREE AT LAST

All hatchlings look like small adults and have to fend for themselves as soon as they hatch. When they are free of the nest, they have to find their way to a suitable habitat. For these leatherback turtle hatchlings, this is the sea. Freshwater turtles sometimes take several days to reach water. Both Blanding's turtle and wood turtle hatchlings follow the trails of others, perhaps picking up their scent.

▲ A BABY IN THE HAND

Baby chelonians are very tiny when they first hatch out. Most are just 30–40mm (1–1$\frac{1}{2}$in) long. These Australian snake-neck turtle hatchlings will easily fit on a person's hand. The one on the left is upside down and the one on the right is the correct way up.

▼ A BIT OF AN ARMFUL!

From left to right these young tortoises are: a red-footed tortoise, an Indian star tortoise, a leopard tortoise and an African spurred tortoise. Different species should not actually be kept together, since they have different habitats and diets and could give each other diseases they would not normally get in the wild. The African spurred tortoise will eventually grow much bigger than all the others – over twice as big as the star tortoise. Some chelonians stop growing when they become adults, but others keep growing throughout their lives.

221

Survival Games

Humans are probably the greatest threat to chelonians, but other predators include alligators, otters, eagles, bears, raccoons, lizards and crabs. Big turtles, such as alligator snappers and Mexican giant musk turtles, also eat some of the smaller mud and musk turtles. Chelonians have many ways of defending themselves against predators. The most obvious ways are withdrawing into the shell, hiding or running away. Vibrations in water or through the ground warn of an approaching enemy, and some chelonians can move away quickly if necessary. Some young chelonians, with their softer shells, have protective spines around the edge of the shell. Few chelonians make it to adulthood, but those who do can live for a long time. Giant tortoises may live for more than 200 years.

▲ STRONG SHELL
The ornate box turtle lives on the vast grasslands or prairies of central North America. It sometimes eats the insects in cattle dung and risks being trampled by cattle hooves as it searches for food. Its high, domed carapace makes the shell stronger, so it is harder to crush than a more flattened shell.

CLEVER CAMOUFLAGE ▶
The pattern on a chelonian's shell often provides good camouflage, which helps it to blend into the surroundings and hide from predators. This Central American wood turtle is very hard to spot among the surrounding brown leaves. Even brightly marked tortoises blend into their natural background surprisingly well, especially when they keep still.

▲ STINKY TURTLE

Stinkpot turtles discourage predators by giving off foul-smelling chemicals from their musk glands – hence their name. Other chelonians that use stinky scent as a form to warn off enemies include common snapping turtles, musk turtles, helmeted terrapins and the gibba turtle from South America.

Did you know? During hibernation, some species spend weeks under water without coming up for air.

▲ SHELL OPENER

Birds of prey, such as this golden eagle, have developed a clever way of breaking open the tough shell of tortoises. They pick the tortoises up in their strong talons (claws) and drop them from a great height on to hard stones or rocks. The force with which the tortoises hit the hard surface may break their shell open. The bird can then eat the soft fleshy body inside the shell.

BUMPS AND SPINES ▶

Some turtles, such as sawback turtles and spiny turtles (right), have bumps and spines on their shells. The bumps of the sawbacks help the turtles tilt the shell to one side if they are flipped over on to their back. This makes it easier for the sawback to right itself again. The spines along the edge of the shell of spiny turtles, especially young ones, probably help with camouflage by breaking up the regular shape of the shell. They also make it very difficult for predators, such as snakes, to swallow them.

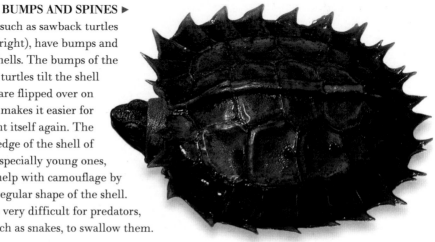

Focus on

Of the seven species of sea turtle, six have hard shells. These are the green, flatback, hawksbill, loggerhead, Kemp's Ridley and olive Ridley turtles. Most of these gentle and mysterious creatures are found in warm waters worldwide. The seventh sea turtle is the leatherback. This soft-shelled giant swims in both warm and cold ocean waters. Sea turtles use their strong flippers to 'fly' through the water. Only the females come on to land to lay their eggs. A male sea turtle may never touch dry land again after hatching from its egg and heading out to sea. In a few places, such as Hawaii, green turtles bask in the sun on beaches.

MYSTERIOUS LIVES
Once a loggerhead hatchling reaches the sea, its movements are not well known. In places such as Florida, they seem to rest on mats of floating seaweed (above). The babies are reddish brown above and below, which gives them good camouflage among the brown seaweed. This helps them to hide from predators.

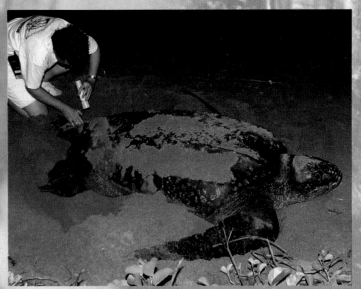

BIGGEST CHELONIAN
This nesting turtle is being observed by a conservation scientist. The enormous leatherback is as long as a tall person and weighs around 659kg (1,450lb). It is the fastest growing of all chelonians, increasing its body weight by about 8,000 times between hatching and growing into an adult. Its shell has no horny scutes. Instead, it has a leathery skin with thousands of small bones embedded in it. It feeds on soft prey such as jellyfish.

Sea Turtles

NESTING TOGETHER

This olive Ridley turtle will join a large group for nesting. More than 100,000 females nest each year on the east coast of India alone. Most sea turtles nest alone or in small groups.

STREAMLINED SHELL

Sea turtles, such as this green sea turtle, have a very streamlined shell to allow the water to flow smoothly over it. They do not have the overhang at the front of the shell, into which other chelonians withdraw their heads, as a ridge would slow a sea turtle down. Instead, its head is protected by thick, horny scales and the solid bony roof of the skull.

AFRICA

ASCENSION ISLAND

SOUTH AMERICA

MIGRATION OF GREEN TURTLES

MIGRATIONS

Sea turtles, both young and adults, swim along ocean migration routes as they move to new feeding sites. Adults also travel to beaches to mate and lay eggs. Scientists are not sure how the turtles find their way. They may smell their route, find their way by the Sun or stars, or use Earth's magnetism.

TORTOISESHELL

The scutes of the hawksbill turtle are a beautiful mixture of amber, brown, black, white, red and green. It is these scutes that are used to make 'tortoiseshell' combs, ornaments and spectacle frames. Sadly, the turtle is usually killed before the scutes are removed. This practice is entirely unnecessary, especially now that so many man-made alternatives are available.

Europe and the Mediterranean

Many tortoises from the area around the Mediterranean Sea belong to the *Testudo* group. This name comes from the Latin word for 'tortoise'. *Testudo* tortoises usually have five claws and all species except *Testudo horsefieldi* have a weak hinge on the plastron. Most tortoises in this group live in dry habitats, although some, such as the European pond turtle and the Spanish turtle, live in water habitats.

The Mediterranean region is a crowded part of the world, and the survival of many of the chelonians in this region is affected by the human population. They are threatened by habitat destruction, disturbance, pollution, summer fires and collection for the pet trade.

▲ **POND LURKER**
The European pond turtle is the only turtle to be found across Europe. A shy omnivore, the pond turtle lives in slow-moving waters with muddy bottoms and overhanging plants. Males have red eyes and longer tails than the yellow-eyed females.

◄ **DRY DWELLER**
Hermann's tortoise is found in dry places across southern Europe, from Spain to Turkey. It also lives on several Mediterranean islands. During the breeding season, rival males may become very aggressive and have shell-ramming contests with each other. The tortoises hibernate between October and April.

SCALY LEGS ▶

The spur-thighed tortoise is found around most of the Mediterranean region and in eastern Europe. In the cooler, northern parts of its range, the tortoise hibernates through winter. In warmer areas, it may be dormant in the hot summer. This is one of the most popular tortoises in the European pet trade, and many have been collected from the wild. Laws have now been passed to try to control this trade.

◀ MIDDLE EASTERN

The Egyptian tortoise lives in the deserts and scrublands of Libya, Egypt and Israel. It shelters from the heat in burrows. This is a very small species, with males having a carapace length of just 10cm (4in) and females being 13cm (5in) long, less than half the size of the marginated tortoise (below). Egyptian tortoises have a yellowish shell and spiky scales on each heel.

Did you know? Legend says that the Greek god Hermes made the first lyre from a tortoise shell.

LOOKING EDGY ▼

The marginated tortoise lives only in southern Greece and on some of its offshore islands. It has been introduced to Sardinia by people. This is the largest of the *Testudo* tortoises, with adults having a carapace length of up to 30cm (12in).

Adults have a very distinctive fringe of flat scutes around the carapace, hence the name 'marginated', meaning 'around the edges, or margins'. Little is known about the habits of this tortoise, but it probably hibernates during the winter in cooler areas.

227

Africa and Madagascar

About 50 species of chelonian live in Africa south of the Sahara Desert and on the island of Madagascar, which lies off the East African coast. Madagascar is home to some interesting and rare tortoises that are found nowhere else in the world, such as the spider tortoise. Unusual chelonians from mainland Africa include the pancake tortoise, hinge-back tortoises and tent tortoises, with their unique shells. These tortoises are adapted to live in dry climates. Africa is also home to many side-necked turtles and softshell turtles, which live in ponds, rivers and marshes.

▲ BIG BURROWER
The African spurred tortoise has a shell that is 75cm (30in) long. Only the giant tortoises of the Galapagos Islands and Aldabra are larger. It lives along the southern edge of the Sahara Desert, in dry grasslands. To avoid the heat and dry air, it hides in burrows during the day and comes out at dusk and dawn, when it is cooler. This tortoise gets most of its water from its food.

▼ PRETTY PATTERNS
The beautiful radiated tortoise lives only in the dry woodland and scrublands of southern Madagascar. It is a relatively large species, growing up to 40cm (16in) long, with a highly domed carapace and a yellowish head. This tortoise lives a long time, with some individuals known to be well over 100 years old. Radiated tortoises are threatened by habitat destruction and other forms of interference, but they are being protected by law and bred in zoos around the world.

◄ A BUMPY ROOF

The spectacular African tent tortoise lives in southern Africa. It survives in various habitats ranging from sandy desert to bushy woodland. The shell varies in shape and pattern. One sub-species catches rain by tipping up the back part of its shell and stretching its front legs and head. Rain flows through the ridges of the shell into the mouth.

▼ CREEPY CRAWLIES

The little Malagasy spider tortoise is named after the pattern of yellow lines on its domed shell that looks like a spider's web. It is the only tortoise with a hinge at the front of the plastron so it can almost close the front of its bottom shell. The spider tortoise lives in forests along the south coast of Madagascar. It is a plant-eater, and it grows up to 15cm (6in) long.

▲ SPECIAL SHELL

African hinge-back tortoises, such as this Bell's hinge-back, can clamp down the back part of the shell tightly to protect their body if they are in danger, often hissing as they do so. Bell's hinge-back lives in dry grasslands where there are wet and dry seasons. It aestivates (stays inactive) during dry seasons, buried in the mud at the bottom of waterholes.

GLORIOUS MUD ►

The West African mud turtle is a side-necked turtle and protects its head by tucking it to the side under its shell. This species lives in a variety of watery habitats, such as rivers, marshes and lakes. If the water dries up for part of the year, these turtles aestivate buried under the mud. The only turtles known to hunt in groups, they will attack and eat water birds.

Asian Chelonians

In many Asian cultures, chelonians are symbols of long life, strength, good fortune and endurance. Live tortoises were presented as gifts to Chinese emperors, and freshwater turtles still live in many temple ponds. Asians also hunt turtles and tortoises for food and for their bones. The bones are used in traditional remedies, especially in China. Unfortunately, many species of chelonians are now close to extinction because too many of them have been collected from the wild for use in these remedies, as well as for food or for sale as pets. Even though protected areas have been set up recently and wildlife protection laws are being enforced more strictly, Asian chelonians still face big survival problems in the future.

▲ DIGGING TORTOISE

Horsfield's tortoise lives further north than any other Asian tortoise. It ranges from Russia to Pakistan, in habitats that are hot in summer but freezing cold in winter. These tortoises dig burrows for shelter with their strong claws. There are laws protecting these tortoises, but they are still sold as pets in many parts of the world.

◀ TURTLE IN A BOX

The shy Malayan box turtle is found throughout South-east Asia. It lives in wetter habitats than the American box turtles, in ponds, marshes and flooded rice fields. This is one of the world's most popular pet species, and so many turtles have been captured from the wild that its numbers have been greatly reduced. This turtle feeds on both plant and animal foods when in captivity, and most likely lives on plants, small fish, water snails and insects in the wild.

▼ ROOFS AND TENTS

The Indian tent turtle belongs to a group of seven species with a carapace that looks like a tent or roof. It is shaped like an arch with a ridge, or keel, running along the middle, with points sticking up from the keel in several species. These Asian tent and roofed turtles look rather like the American sawback turtles. Their toes are webbed for swimming.

▲ RARE IMPRESSIONS

The rare impressed tortoise has an unusual flat carapace covered with scutes that have a dip in the middle. It lives in dry forests on hills in South-east Asia and China. These tortoises rely on heavy dew or wet plants for drinking water. They are very difficult to keep in captivity and are endangered due to hunting as well as habitat destruction.

▼ INDIAN FLAP-SHELL TURTLE

Hunted for its meat and for the pet trade, the Indian spotted flap-shell is gravely endangered. It is one of the smallest of the softshell turtles; males are only 15cm (6in) long. As with all softshells, there are three claws on each foot. This species lives in the shallow and still waters of rivers, marshes, ponds, lakes and canals. It aestivates during dry periods.

Tortoise Guardian
This bronze sculpture of a tortoise is in the Forbidden City in Beijing, China. The tortoise symbolized long life, wisdom and happiness for the emperors who ruled China. In Chinese mythology, the tortoise is one of four spiritual creatures, each guarding a direction of the compass. The tortoise is guardian of the north, a bird guards the south, a dragon guards the east and a tiger guards the west. These four animals also represent the four seasons – the tortoise represents winter. For over 4,000 years, tortoise shells have been used in Chinese rituals to foretell the future.

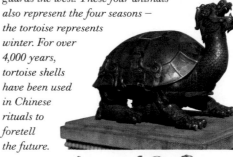

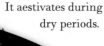

231

American Chelonians

North, Central and South America are home to a vast variety of chelonians, ranging from common species, such as cooters and sliders, to rarer species, such as the Arrau river turtle and the matamata. One species, the Central American river turtle, looks just like its relatives that lived millions of years ago. It is so well adapted to its underwater environment that it has not needed to change over time.

As with chelonians in many other places, American ones are threatened by hunting and habitat destruction. Galapagos tortoises have the added problem of goats, which were introduced to the islands by humans and compete with the tortoises for food.

▲ TASTY TURTLE
The chicken turtle used to be a popular food in the southern United States and gets its popular name from its succulent flesh. It is common in still water, such as ponds and swamps. In the wild, its shell often becomes thickly coated with algae.

COMMON COOTERS ►
Cooters are large freshwater turtles with a carapace measuring up to 40cm (16in) long. Males are slightly smaller and flatter than females. They have long claws on the front feet which they use for stroking the female during their courtship display. Florida cooters like to bask in the sunshine, and groups of as many as 20 or 30 individuals may bask together. Each female lays two clutches of about 20 eggs each year, and the hatchlings are very brightly patterned.

▲ SPINY SOFTSHELL

The habitat of the strange-looking spiny softshell turtle ranges across most of North America and down into Mexico. The round carapace measures about 50cm (20in) long and has a rough, leathery covering. The spiny softshell turtle spends most of its time in the water, often burying itself in sandy river bottoms. In shallow water, it may be able to stretch out its neck to breathe at the water's surface, while remaining hidden in the sand. Its prey includes fish, frogs and crayfish.

▼ TWIST-NECKED TURTLE

The twist-necked turtle from northern South America is a side-necked turtle and lives in shallow rainforest streams and pools. It also wanders about the forest floor after rain. Since it is a poor swimmer, it does not live in large, fast-flowing rivers. The female does not dig a nesting hole, but lays one egg at a time under rotten leaves on the ground.

◄ HOOKED JAWS

The narrow-bridge musk turtle, from Central America, has several unusual features. One of the most obvious is the long hook on the bottom jaw and the tooth-like points on the top jaw. These formidable jaws help it to catch prey, such as frogs, fish and worms. Although quite shy, this turtle can give people a nasty bite if provoked. There are hardly any scales on the skin, and the plastron is very small, with only seven bones.

RED-FOOTED TORTOISE ►

Unlike most tortoises, the South American red-footed tortoise is very decorative, with bright red scales on the head, legs and tail and yellow spots on the shell. Males have longer, thicker tails than females. They also have a dip in the plastron, which helps them to climb on top of the more rounded female's carapace to mate. During mating, the males make clucking sounds.

Focus on

FOOD WITH DRINK
This desert tortoise is eating the fruit of a prickly pear cactus, a plant with a lot of water stored inside. Desert tortoises also eat wildflowers and grasses, often sniffing or sampling plants before they bite. Sometimes they eat soil, which provides the bacteria needed to help them break down their food. They swallow small stones, called gastroliths, which crush plant food as they churn round in the tortoise's stomach.

AMERICAN DESERTS
The desert tortoise of North and Central America lives in the Mojave and Sonoran deserts of south-eastern California, Arizona and Mexico. Today its habitat is under threat from land development, off-road vehicles and grazing farm animals. Many non-desert plants have taken root in the area. This is not good news for the tortoises, which need to feed on native plants to stay healthy.

Tortoises living in the deserts of North and Central America and Africa get most of their water from the plants they eat. They may also catch rainwater on their shell or dig basins to collect rainwater during showers. If water is not available, desert tortoises can absorb some of the water stored in their bladder. They may also survive a year or more without water. They tend to be active in the cool of the morning and evening. The hottest times of day, and very hot or cold seasons, are spent resting, aestivating or hibernating in underground burrows. These burrows are more moist and cooler than the surface of the desert.

Desert Tortoises

SUMMER SIESTA

The North American desert tortoise spends hot summer seasons, when food and water are hard to find, asleep in its burrow. During this 'summer sleep', or aestivation, the tortoise's body processes keep working normally, even though it hardly moves at all. This is different from its 'winter sleep', or hibernation, when its body processes slow down.

BORROWED BURROWS

The little Egyptian tortoise does not dig its own burrows, but uses burrows dug by rodents. This helps it to avoid hot temperatures. The Egyptian tortoise is rare, because it is threatened by the disturbance of its habitat. There are fewer and fewer bushes remaining, which are needed by desert rodents. This means there are fewer rodent burrows for the tortoise to shelter in.

CHAMPION DIGGER

The flattened, muscular front legs of the desert tortoise are brilliant tools for digging burrows that can be over 10m (33ft) long. The female uses her back legs for digging nest holes, too. She digs by scraping at the soil first with one leg and then the other. When the hole becomes deep enough, the tortoise turns around and pushes the dirt out with her shoulders.

Australasian Chelonians

Australia has been isolated from the rest of the world for millions of years, and this has allowed some rare and unusual species of chelonians to develop. The pig-nosed turtle is found only in this region, as are snake-necked turtles. Other chelonians in the same family as the snake-necked turtles include the river turtles and the snapping turtles of Australia and New Guinea. As with chelonians elsewhere in the world, many Australasian ones are very rare, but two species are especially so. The western swamp turtle lives only in pools near Perth, and the Fitzroy River turtle lives in only one river system in Queensland.

▲ SWIMMING PIG

An agile swimmer, the pig-nosed turtle has many unique features, including a pointed nose, a leathery shell and flipper-like limbs. It also has crescent-shaped scales along the top of its tail. The pig-nosed turtle rarely leaves the water but may bask on floating objects. It has a varied diet, including plants, insects and fish.

◄ SNAKE-NECKED TURTLES

With their extraordinary long necks, snake-necked turtles make rapid, snake-like strikes at their prey. They are active and very efficient predators, catching prey such as fish, shrimps, tadpoles and frogs. Some even manage to catch water birds. Like all side-necked turtles, snake-necked turtles tuck their long neck sideways under their shell to avoid danger or intense heat.

EASTERN TURTLE ▶

Basking on a log in the sun are two eastern river turtles, also called Brisbane short-necked turtles. They live in the east of Australia. Eastern river turtles have sensitive chin barbels and a yellow spot on each side of the chin. Adult males have flatter carapaces than females and longer, thicker tails.

◀ **SERRATED SNAP**

Beware of the serrated snapping turtle! It defends itself by snapping and biting and may also release a foul-smelling liquid from its musk glands. The serrated part of its name comes from the jagged edge on the back of its carapace. Younger ones have a ridge, or a keel, along the top of their shell. The serrated snapping turtle is a side-necked turtle, but it has a much shorter neck than its close relatives the snake-necked turtles. Males have much longer tails than females.

Aboriginal Art

This tortoise was painted on the rocks by Aboriginal people in Kakadu National Park, northern Australia. Aboriginal rock art can be up to 40,000 years old and was painted for a number of reasons, such as to ensure a successful hunt, to record ceremonies, to change events and people's lives through sorcery and magic, and to tell stories about the Creation Ancestors. Long ago, during the 'Dreamtime', these ancestors were believed to have created the landscape and every living creature before changing into land forms, animals, stars or other objects. The act of painting puts artists in touch with their Creation Ancestors and is seen as an important and powerful experience in itself.

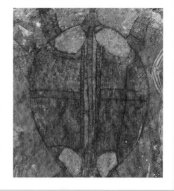

Ancient Chelonians

▲ FORMING FOSSILS
This fossil tortoise was found in the
badlands of South Dakota, in the
United States. It lived about 35 million
years ago, when that area was covered
in a shallow sea. Rock and minerals
have filled in the spaces inside the
tortoise's shell and then turned into
hard stone, preserving the tortoise's
body for millions of years.

Scientists have different ideas about which
group of animals chelonians evolved from.
The oldest known chelonian, called
Odontochelys, lived about 220 million years
ago, but this ancient turtle probably did
not give rise to modern chelonians. These
are most likely to have developed from a
group called the Casichelydia, which lived
between 208 and 144 million years ago.
Ancient chelonians lived alongside the
dinosaurs – giant reptiles that roamed the
Earth until 65 million years ago, when
they all died out. Unlike the dinosaurs,
many chelonian species survived and are
still around today.

▶ LARGEST TURTLE
About 100 million years ago there was an ancient turtle called *Archelon*,
which was bigger than a rowing boat. It swam in an
inland sea that once covered the grassy prairies of
North America. *Archelon* looked like modern
leatherback turtles, with a leathery,
streamlined carapace and wing-like
front flippers. It had very weak
jaws and may have fed on
jellyfish and other animals
with soft bodies, such as
squid. The most complete
fossil of *Archelon* is of an
animal that was about
100 years old when it
died. It was 4.5m (15ft)
long and 5.25m (17ft)
from one outstretched
front flipper to the other.

Triassic 252–201mya	Jurassic 201–145mya	Cretaceous 145–66mya	Paleogene to present 66mya to present		mya – millions of years ago
			Trionychoidea (Cretaceous–recent)	Kinosternidae	Mud or musk turtles
				Dermatemydidae	Central American river turtle
Odontochelys (extinct)				Carettochelyidae	Pig-nosed turtle
	Cryptodira (Late Jurassic)		Chelonioidea (Jurassic–recent)	Trionychidae	Softshell turtles
				Dermochelyidae	Leatherback turtle
	Casichelydia (dominant during Jurassic)			Cheloniidae	Sea turtles
			Testudinoidea (Paleocene–recent)	Chelydridae	Snapping turtles
				Platysternidae	Big-headed turtle
				Emydidae	Pond turtles and relatives
				Testudinidae	Land tortoises
			Pleurodira (Late Cretaceous–recent)	Chelidae	Austro-South American side-necked turtles
				Pelomedusidae	African side-necked turtles

▲ EVOLUTION PATHWAYS

This diagram shows how chelonians may have evolved over a period of 220 million years. A group called the Casichelydia became dominant about 208 million years ago and gave rise to the 12 families of chelonians alive today. They are listed to the top right of the chart above.

Island Evolution

On the Galapagos Islands the English scientist Charles Darwin found some of the most important evidence for his theory of how evolution happens. During his visit in 1835 he collected information about how the giant tortoises and other animals varied between islands. He suggested that these differences had come about because the animals had adapted to suit the unique conditions on each island.

The best-adapted animals survived to produce the next generation, an idea that Darwin called 'natural selection'.

▲ SNAPPING FOSSILS

This is a fossil of a young snapping turtle that lived between 58 and 37 million years ago. You can see the outline of its shell and its long tail. From fossils, we know that there were more species of snapping turtles in the past. Today only the common snapping turtle and the alligator snapping turtle are still alive.

239

Chelonian Relatives

The closest relatives of chelonians alive today are other reptiles, a name that means 'creeping creatures'. Reptiles have a bony skeleton, a backbone and scaly skin. They rely on their surroundings for warmth and are most common in warmer places. Reptiles lay eggs with waterproof shells or give birth to live young. The main groups of living reptiles are: turtles and tortoises, lizards and snakes, and crocodiles and alligators. Chelonians look very different from other reptiles. They also have no holes in the roof of their skull, while all other reptiles have two openings there.

▲ LEGLESS WONDER
With their long and slender, bendy bodies, snakes, such as this rattlesnake, look nothing like chelonians, despite evolving from a common ancestor. They have no legs, no eyelids and no external ears. Snakes have a forked tongue for tasting and for smelling the air. All snakes are meat-eaters and swallow their prey whole. They evolved much later than chelonians, between 100 and 150 million years ago, but have developed into many more species – about 2,700 different kinds in total.

▼ AMAZING ALLIGATORS
Alligators are large and fierce predators that belong to the crocodilian group of reptiles, which includes 13 species of alligator, crocodile, caiman and gharial. These long-snouted monsters have powerful jaws lined with sharp teeth. They are all meat-eaters, tackling prey of all sizes from fish to zebras. Although they live in or near fresh water or the sea, crocodilians must lay their eggs on land, just like chelonians.

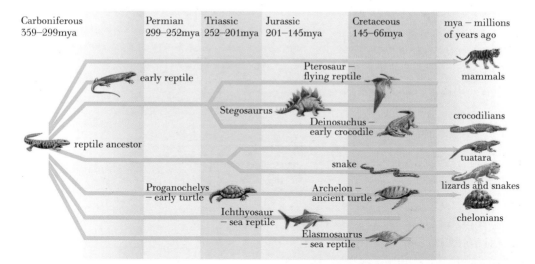

Carboniferous 359–299mya	Permian 299–252mya	Triassic 252–201mya	Jurassic 201–145mya	Cretaceous 145–66mya	mya – millions of years ago

early reptile

reptile ancestor

Pterosaur – flying reptile

Stegosaurus

Deinosuchus – early crocodile

snake

Proganochelys – early turtle

Ichthyosaur – sea reptile

Archelon – ancient turtle

Elasmosaurus – sea reptile

mammals

crocodilians

tuatara

lizards and snakes

chelonians

▲ REPTILE EVOLUTION

The first reptiles evolved from amphibians about 300 million years ago and looked like small lizards. About 220 million years ago, chelonians appeared and branched away from the other reptiles. These others then divided into two main groups: snakes and lizards, and the archosaurs, which includes dinosaurs, crocodiles and extinct flying reptiles called pterosaurs.

LIVING FOSSIL ▼

The tuatara is an unusual reptile that has changed so little since the days of the dinosaurs that people refer to it as a 'living fossil'. Today there are just two species of tuatara, living on islands off the coast of New Zealand. They are burrowing reptiles that live in coastal forests and come out at night. Tuataras live for a long time, probably over 100 years. This long lifespan is something they have in common with chelonians.

▲ LOTS OF LIZARDS

There are more species of lizard than any other group of reptiles – over 4,000 of them. This is a very unusual lizard from the Galapagos Islands. It is an iguana that lives on the seashore and dives under the water to graze on seaweed.

241

Chelonians and People

People are not good news for chelonians. They destroy, build on and pollute the places where these reptiles live. People also often introduce new animals into their habitats, such as goats and rats, that eat all the chelonians' plant food or eat their eggs. Chelonians are also caught for food or killed in fishing nets by accident. Their shells and skins are used to make trinkets, and other body parts are used in medicines. When people handle chelonians, they may pass on diseases that kill them. Catching wild chelonians to sell as pets reduces the numbers left in the wild, and many die before they reach the shop. Some pets are also neglected and do not live long.

▲ NO PLACE TO LIVE

The places where chelonians once lived are fast disappearing, as human populations expand rapidly and towns, roads and farms replace natural habitats. Many chelonians are run over as they plod their way slowly across roads. Desert tortoises are threatened by off-road vehicles. Even in the oceans, oil rigs and boat traffic badly affect sea turtles.

FOOD AND HUNTING ▶

Chelonians are relatively easy for people to catch as they move so slowly. Some traditional hunters, such as this San woman from southern Africa, use the meat as an important food source for their families. Catching small numbers is not a problem, however, as enough survive to replace those caught. Over-hunting to sell chelonians for high prices as gourmet food, for tortoiseshell or as live specimens to animal collectors is still a big problem. Much of the hunting is illegal and hard to control.

◀ CAUGHT IN THE NET

Commercial fishing nets often scoop up sea turtles, such as this baby hawksbill, as they are pulled through the oceans. The turtles become entangled in the nets and are strangled or drown, since they cannot reach the surface to breathe air. In 1999, 150,000 turtles were killed in this way by the shrimp-fishing industry all over the world. Sea turtles also get tangled up in long-lines, which are deep-water fishing lines many miles long with thousands of baited hooks.

PET CHELONIANS ▶

Many people like to keep chelonians, such as land tortoises or terrapins, as pets. This is, however, not a decision to be taken lightly, as they can live for a very long time. They also need to be treated with care and respect and given appropriate food and housing. People can also pick up some diseases from chelonians, and vice versa. Most turtles in the pet trade are still taken from the wild, although some are bred in captivity, such as these baby wood turtles.

▼ EGGS FOR SALE

These green-turtle eggs are being sold in a market in Malaysia. They cost more than chicken eggs, and in some areas they are used in love potions. If too many eggs are taken from the wild, there will not be enough baby turtles for the future.

▲ TOURIST SOUVENIRS

In some countries, turtles and tortoises are still killed and their shells are made into souvenirs. The skin of Pacific and olive Ridley turtles is used to make soft leather items. The rest of the turtle is thrown away or used for pet food, hot dogs or fertilizer. If people stopped buying products made from turtles and tortoises, then this sad, and often illegal, industry would end.

Focus on

Turtles and tortoises are in terrible trouble. Populations nearly everywhere are shrinking, and many species are threatened or vulnerable. Over half of the world's chelonians are currently facing the threat of extinction, and unless we do more to save them now, countless species will be lost in the near future. Chelonians have no way of defending themselves against people, and they are too easy for us to catch. Females nest only in certain areas and at regular times, so people can easily harvest their eggs and young. Since they grow so slowly and take a long time to mature and reproduce, it is difficult for chelonians to build up their numbers again once they have been reduced to low levels.

ANGONOKA TORTOISE

This is one of the most endangered species in the world. Only a few hundred individuals survive in one area of Madagascar. These rare animals are now being bred in zoos around the world.

AFRICAN RARITY

The beautiful geometric tortoise has lost 96 per cent of its habitat because of agriculture, development and frequent wildfires. It was once more widespread but now lives in the south-western tip of South Africa. Here it inhabits isolated patches of a unique mixture of grasses and short, dry shrubs, which grow on acidic, sandy soils.

Rare Chelonians

ENDANGERED EUROPEAN
For centuries European pond turtles have been captured for food or destroyed because people considered them harmful to fish. Recent problems facing these turtles include pollution and the building of embankments along waterways, which stop the turtles from moving about freely to find food or mates.

SMUGGLING TORTOISES
Despite its name, the Egyptian tortoise is almost extinct in Egypt. Even though there are laws banning selling these tortoises, smuggling still occurs. This tortoise is rare not only because of habitat destruction and disturbance but also because of pet traders collecting them from the wild.

PROTECTING PANCAKES
The increasingly rare pancake tortoise lives only in Kenya and Tanzania in East Africa. It is threatened by people using its habitat for farming and by poaching for the pet trade. Even though these tortoises are protected by law and Kenya bans their export, smuggling occurs. Many of these unusual tortoises have died on journeys to other parts of the world. Since pancake tortoises lay only one egg at a time, it is hard for them to replace their numbers if too many are taken from the wild.

Conservation

Even though chelonians have survived on the Earth for hundreds of millions of years, their future survival is uncertain. We need to find out much more about how they live in the wild, so that we can work out the best ways to help them. One thing we do know for sure is that they need all the help they can get. Conservation measures to help chelonians include preserving their habitats, stopping illegal poaching and smuggling, controlling the pet trade, and breeding rare species in captivity so that they can be released back into the wild. Many countries have laws to protect chelonians, but these are difficult to enforce, especially in developing countries with fewer resources.

▲ PROTECTED BREEDING
On this Malaysian beach, the sticks mark the positions of leatherback turtle eggs buried in the sand. Within this protected area, the eggs are cared for and the hatchlings are helped on their journey to the sea. Populations of leatherbacks have declined drastically. The causes include people taking eggs from nests, and adults being caught in fishing nets at sea.

GATHERING DATA ▶
The loggerhead migrates thousands of miles each year, but scientists are not sure how it finds its way. The transmitter fixed to the shell of this loggerhead turtle will allow scientists to track its movements through the ocean. Every time the turtle comes to the surface for air, a signal is sent via a satellite to a research team. This tells the scientists where the turtles are, what the water temperature is and so on. Transmitters fixed to land chelonians are also providing information about how these tortoises live. The data gathered can be used to help protect species and preserve their limited habitats.

TORTOISE TRUST ▶

Organizations such as the Tortoise Trust campaign for the protection of turtles and tortoises around the world. The Tortoise Trust is the world's largest chelonian organization, active in more than 26 countries. It gives advice on how to care for pet chelonians, promotes research and helps to find good homes for turtles and tortoises in need.

▲ BROUGHT UP SAFELY

Captive breeding of seriously endangered species, such as this Australian western swamp tortoise, may be the only way to save them from extinction. It is not always easy to breed chelonians in captivity, as they may suffer from stress and disease. Even if the breeding scheme is a success, there may not be a suitable area of their wild habitat left to release them into once they are mature.

▼ ECO-TOURISM

In some places tourists can help to save rare chelonians by going to watch them, as these tourists are doing in the Galapagos Islands. The money they pay can go towards conservation schemes. These tourists must be carefully controlled so they do not upset the chelonians or pass on any diseases. Unfortunately, the noise and disruption from tourists on sea turtle nesting beaches can confuse and disturb females so that they go back to sea without laying their eggs.

▼ CONTROLLING TRADE

The international pet trade condemns many chelonians to a slow and miserable death after collecting them from the wild. They are often packed tightly together in crates, such as this one seized by customs officials in Vietnam. With hardly any space, and no food or water, a large number of animals die during their journey.

GLOSSARY

aestivation
A period of rest during heat and drought, similar to hibernation.

albino
An animal that lacks coloration on all or part of its body and which belongs to a species that is not usually so.

amphisbaenian
A legless reptile that has evolved from the lizards.

anaconda
A type of boa.

antivenin
A substance made from snake venom and/or the blood of mammals that is used to treat snakebites.

arid
Very dry.

bacteria
A large group of microscopic, single-celled living organisms.

barbel
A sensitive finger of skin under the chin of some chelonians.

bask
To lie in the warmth of the sun.

bifurcated tail
A V-shaped tail that is formed when one tail does not fully come off and a second tail then grows from the wound.

billabong
Branch of a river that comes to a dead end in a backwater or stagnant pool.

bird of prey
A predatory bird with sharp claws and a hooked beak, such as an eagle or falcon, that hunts animals.

boas
A group of snakes that live mainly in North and South America. They give birth to live young and kill by squeezing their prey.

brille
A transparent scale covering a snake's eye. It is also called a spectacle.

camouflage
Pigments or patterns that help an animal blend into its surroundings.

canine
A sharp, pointed tooth next to the incisors that grips and pierces the skin of prey.

carapace
The top part of a chelonian's shell.

carcass
The dead body of an animal.

carettochelyidae
A chelonian family with only one species, which is the pig-nosed turtle.

carnivore
An animal that eats meat and fish.

carrion
Animals that have been dead for some time.

chelidae
A family of side-necked turtles from South America and the Australia-New Guinea region.

chelonians
Reptiles with bony shells and sharp, horny jaws. The term includes all turtles, tortoises and terrapins.

cheloniidae
A chelonian family that contains six species of sea turtles: green, flatback, loggerhead, Kemp's Ridley, olive Ridley and hawksbill.

chelydridae
A family of snapping turtles, which contains two species: the alligator snapping turtle and common snapping turtle.

classification
Grouping of animals according to their similarities and differences in order to study them. This also suggests how they may have developed over time.

cloaca
Combined opening of the end of the gut, the reproductive system and the urinary system in reptiles, amphibians and birds.

clutch
A set of eggs that are laid and incubated together.

cobras
Venomous snakes in the elapid family, with short, fixed fangs at the front of the mouth.

cold-blooded
An animal whose temperature varies with that of its surroundings.

colony
A large group of animals of the same species living together.

colubrids
Mostly harmless snakes. These snakes make up the biggest group nearly three-quarters of the world's snakes.

compost heap
A pile of layers of garden plants, leaves and soil. Compost gives off heat as it rots down and can eventually be dug into the soil to make it rich.

conservation
Protecting living things and helping them to survive.

constrictor
A snake that kills by coiling its body tightly around its prey to suffocate it.

courtship
Ritual displays that take place before mating.

crocodilian
A member of the group of animals that includes crocodiles, alligators, caimans and gharials.

crustacean
A type of invertebrate such as crabs, slaters or woodlice.

dewlap
A flap of skin under the chin, often brightly pigmented and used for display.

dermochelyidae
A chelonian family that has only one species, the leatherback sea turtle.

diaphragm
A sheet of muscle separating the chest cavity from the abdominal cavity, the movement of which helps with breathing.

diapsid
A type of skull with two openings on either side, behind the eye socket.

digestion
The process by which food is broken down so that it can be absorbed into the body.

digit
Finger or toe at the end of an animal's limb.

dinosaur
An extinct group of reptiles that lived from 245 to 65 million years ago and dominated life on Earth.

dominant animal
An animal that the other members of its group allow to take first place.

eardrum
Part of the ear that vibrates when sound hits it.

ectotherm
A cold-blooded animal.

egg tooth
A small tooth in the front of a baby reptile's mouth, which helps it to break free from its eggshell.

elapids
A group of venomous snakes that includes the cobras, mambas and the coral snakes. Elapids live in hot countries.

emydidae
A large and varied family of pond turtles including: the painted terrapin, spiny turtle, Indian tent turtle, wood turtle and diamond-back terrapin.

endangered
A species that is likely to die out in the near future.

epidermis
The outer layer of the skin.

estuary
The mouth of a large river where it reaches the sea.

evolution
The process by which living things adapt over generations to changes in their surroundings.

extinct
When every member of a species of animal or plant dies out.

fang
A long, pointed tooth that may be used to deliver venom.

flipper
A leg that has adapted into a flat blade for swimming.

fossils
The preserved remains of living things, usually found in rocks.

gall bladder
A small organ attached to the liver.

gastroliths
Hard objects, such as stones, swallowed by crocodilians, that stay in the stomach to help crush food.

gator
A shortened name for an alligator, commonly used in the USA.

gizzard
A muscular chamber in an animal's gut that grinds large lumps of food into small pieces or particles.

habitat
The type of place where an animal naturally lives.

hard-tongued lizards
All lizards not contained in the group Iguania.

herbivore
An animal that eats only plants.

hibernation
A long period of inactivity when all body processes are slowed down in very cold weather.

Iguania
The name given to the group of lizards containing iguanas, agamas, chameleons, anoles, swift lizards, lava lizards, basilisks and spiny lizards.

incubation
Using heat to help eggs develop.

infrasounds
Very low sounds that are too low for people to hear.

intestines
Part of an animal's gut where food is broken down and absorbed into the body.

invertebrate
An animal without a backbone.

Jacobson's organ
A sensitive organ in the roof of the mouth into which the tongue places scent particles.

juvenile
A young animal before it grows and develops into a mature adult.

keratin
A horny substance that makes up the scales of lizards, snakes and tuataras.

kinosternidae
A chelonian family of mud and musk turtles including: the loggerhead musk turtle and narrow-bridged musk turtle.

mammal
An animal with fur or hair and a backbone, which can control its own body temperature. All female mammals feed their young on milk.

marine
Sea-living or sea-going.

mature
Developed enough to be capable of reproduction.

membrane
A thin film, skin or layer.

microbes
Living things such as bacteria too small to see with the naked eye.

migration
A regular journey to find food, water or a place to breed or lay eggs.

molar
A chewing and grinding tooth at the side of the jaw.

molluscs
Invertebrates with hard shells, such as mussels, clams or snails.

moulting
The process by which a snake sheds its skin.

navigating
Finding the way to a certain place.

nictitating membrane
A third eyelid that can be passed over the eye to keep it clean or shield it.

omnivore
An animal that eats all kinds of food, both plants and animals.

osteoderms
Rigid plates that add strength to a lizard's skin.

palate
The roof of the mouth. An extra or secondary bony palate separates the mouth from the breathing passages.

parasite
A living thing that lives on or inside another living thing and does not benefit its host.

pelomedusidae
A family of side-necked turtles found in South America, Madagascar, Africa and the Seychelles, including: the West African mud turtle, African forest turtle and giant South American river turtle.

pigment
Coloured matter
in the skin.

pits
Heat sensors located on either
side of a snake's head.

plastron
The flat, bottom part of a
chelonian's shell.

platysternidae
A chelonian family with just one
species, the big-
headed turtle.

poaching
Capturing and/or killing animals
illegally and selling them for
commercial gain.

pod
A group of young crocodilians
just out of their eggs.

predator
An animal that hunts and kills
other animals for food.

prehensile
Able to grip.

prehistoric
Dating from long ago, before
people kept historical records.

prey
An animal that is hunted and
eaten by other animals.

pupil
The dark opening in the middle
of the eye that allows light
to enter.

python
A group of snakes that lives
mainly in Australia, Africa
and Asia. Pythons lay eggs.
They kill their prey
by constriction.

rainforest
The tropical forest that
grows near the equator,
where it is hot and wet
all year round.

range
The maximum area in which
an animal roams.

rattlesnakes
Snakes that live mainly in the
south-western United States
and in Mexico. They have a
warning rattle made of empty
tail sections at the end of
the tail.

reptile
A scaly, cold-blooded animal
with a backbone, including
tortoises, turtles, snakes, lizards
and crocodiles.

rodent
An animal such as a rat, mouse
or squirrel, with chisel-shaped
incisors (front teeth) used
for gnawing.

saliva
A transparent liquid produced by
glands in the mouth. Saliva helps
to slide food from the mouth to
the throat. In some snakes, saliva
also aids digestion.

salivary gland
Gland opening into or near the
mouth that produces the fluids
in the mouth that start the
process of breaking food down
for digestion.

scavenger
An animal that feeds on
carrion.

scutes
Horny scales that cover the shells
of chelonians and the bodies of
crocodilians.

slash and burn
Cutting down and burning
forests to create farmland.

sloughing
Shedding skin. Lizards slough
when a new layer of epidermis
has grown beneath the old skin.

solar panel
An electric device that turns
heat and light from the sun into
electric power.

251

species
A group of animals that share the same characteristics and can breed with one another to produce fertile young.

spurs
Leg bones attached to the hip bones, which are found in boas and pythons and used during courtship displays.

streamlined
A smooth, slim shape that cuts through air or water easily.

succulent
A plant that stores water in its stem or leaves.

swamp
A waterlogged area of land or forest, such as the mangrove swamps found in Florida, USA.

territory
An area of land that one or more animals defend against members of the same species and other species.

testudinidae
A chelonian family of land tortoises, including: the leopard tortoise, impressed tortoise, Galapagos giant tortoise and radiated tortoise.

trionychidae
A chelonian family of soft-shelled turtles, including: the Florida softshell turtle, spiny softshell turtle and Zambezi flapshell turtle.

tropics
The hot regions or countries near the equator and between the Tropic of Cancer and the Tropic of Capricorn.

tuataras
Lizard-like animals that have their own separate reptile group. Today there are only two living species in New Zealand.

venom
Toxic fluid produced by two lizards, the Gila monster and the beaded lizard, for defending against predators. This is also produced in the glands of some snakes to kill their prey.

vertebrate
An animal with a backbone.

vipers
A group of highly venomous snakes with fangs that fold. Some vipers have heat pits on their faces. Most vipers give birth to live young.

viviparous
Gives birth to live young rather than laying eggs.

vocal cords
Two folds of skin in the throats of warm-blooded animals that vibrate and produce sound when air passes through them.

warm-blooded
An animal that can maintain its body at roughly the same warm temperature all the time.

warning colours
Bright shades that show others that an animal is poisonous or venomous. Such patterns also warn predators to keep away.

windpipe
In air-breathing animals, the breathing tube that leads from the mouth opening to the lungs.

yolk sac
A bag of food that is rich in protein and fats, located inside an egg. It nourishes a developing embryo.

INDEX

PICTURE CREDITS
b=bottom, t=top, c=central, l=left, r=right

SNAKES

Jane Burton/Warren Photographic: pages 35c, 46–7 and 54tr; Bruce Coleman Ltd: pages 12bl, 14bl, 20br, 21r, 22tl, 23tl, 24tl, 25cr, 26cl, 26tr, 26br, 27tr, 27bl, 28br, 33br, 34t, 35b, 36br, 37t, 39cr, 39bl, 39r, 40bl, 42c, 43bl, 45br, 50cl, 50br, 52bl, 52br, 54tr, 54cr, 54b, 56cr, 56b, 59tr, 60bl, 62bl, 62cr, 65br, 66tr and 67b; Ecoscene: pages 23cr and 65tl; Mary Evans Picture Library: pages 51tr and 59br; FLPA: pages 17cr, 17cl, 22c, 24b, 29tl, 29tr, 32tl, 32c, 37cr, 38–9, 41tr, 41bl, 44cr, 45t, 45bl, 46–7, 49tr, 51cl, 51br, 54cl, 57bl, 56–7, 58b, 58r, 61tl, 63bl and 66br; Holt Studios International: pages 28tl, 52tr and 64tl; Nature Photographers: page 36bc; NHPA: pages 13bl, 14tl, 15tr, 15bl, 17tl, 20tl, 24br, 25tl, 25br, 28bl, 29bl, 29br, 37cl, 42–3, 43tr, 43cr, 44bl, 48cl, 53tl, 53cl, 53bl, 55cl, 55r, 56tl, 57t and 59c; Oxford Scientific Films: pages 12tc, 18–9, 30–1, 48t, 49b and 62br; Planet Earth Pictures: pages 34b, 38cl, 38br, 38tr, 44tr, 48br, 49c, 60tr, 60br, 61cr, 63cr, 66cl, 67tl and 67tr; Visual Arts Library: pages 11br, 11br and 33bl; Zefa Pictures: page 57br. Special photography: Kim Taylor/Warren Photographic: pages 10–11, 13tr, 16bl, 16bc, 17tr, 18–19, 20–21, 22cl, 22bl, 30–1, 33tr, 35t, 37bl, 40tl, 40–1, 41cr, 42bl, 43r, 58cl, 62tr, 63t, 64b, 65c, 59bl.

CROCODILES

ABPL: 101t/C Haagner, 71c, 88b/C Hughes, 94b/M Harvey, 71tl,84bl/R de la Harper, 102b,103t/S Adev, 89b; Ancient Art & Architecture Collection, 108br; BBC Natural History Unit: /A Shah, 91t/J Rotman, 76bl/M Barton, 74bl/P Oxford, 115br/T Pooley, 101c; Biofotos: /B Rogers, 109t; Adam Britton: 79br, 83bl, 89cl, 92tr, 93cl, 95cr, 101br, 114tr; Bruce Coleman: /Animal Ark, 113tl/CB&DW Frith, 121br/E&P Bauer, 122b/G Cozzi, 104b /J McDonald, 113c/LC Marigo, 105bl, 107br, 112t, 115c/M Plage, 118c/R Williams, 72br; CM Dixon: 74br; e.t. archive: 92bl; FLPA: /G Lacz, 97tl/W Wisniewski, 82b; Heather Angel: 85cr, 126b; M&P Fogden: 80t, 87bl, 94t, 112c, 99cl, 113b, 124t; Mary Evans Picture Library: 70bl, 86br, 107bl; Natural History Museum, London: 116b, 117c; Nature Photographers Ltd/EA James, 76br/R Tidman, 75b/SC Bisserot, 92br; NHPA: 104t, 118t/D Heuchlin, 77c, 89t, 100t, 103c, 111(both), 124b, 125tr, 125b, 127tl/E Soder, 121bl/H&V Ingen, 75bl/ J Shaw, 115t/K Schafer, 93t/M Harvey, 86bl/M Wendler, 71tr, 107c, 123cr, 128tr, 127b/N Wu, 93b/ NJ Dennis, 105cl, 127c/O Rogge, 82tl/P Scott, 124c/S Robinson, 81br; Oxford Scientific Films/A Bee, 121tr/B Wright, 77tr/Breck P Kent, 125tl/E Robinson, 70tr, 96b/ER Degginger, 73cr/F Ehrenstrom, 72tr/F Schneidermeyer, 81cl/F Whitehead, 106t/J Macdonald, 75c/J McCammon,

122t/J Robinson, 86tl/K Westerkov, 118b/M Deeble&V Stone, 83tl, 85cl, 88tl, 95t, 95b, 99b, 102t, 105cr/M Fogden, 81tl/M Pitts, 114b; endpapers/M Sewell, 74t/O Newman, 107t/R Davies, 109b/S Leszczynski, 81cr, 119b, 123t/S Osolinski, 72bl, 78tr, 96t, 97cl, 109c/S Turner, 115bl/W Shattil, 87t; Planet Earth: /A&M Shah, 91c/B Kenney, 100b/C Farnetti, 98b/D Kjaer, 105tl/D Maitland, 106b/DA Ponton, 85b/G Bell, 89c/J Lythgoe, 98t/J Scott, 83tr, 90bl, 91b, 97bl/JA Provenza, 84tr/K Lucas, 70–1, 77bl, 110t, 119tl(both), 123cl,/M&C Denis-Huot, 80cl/N Greaves, 90tl/P Stephenson, 126t/R de la Harper, 99tl, 108t, 112b; Survival Anglia: /F Koster, 110b/M Linley, 120t/M Price, 108bl/V Sinha, 75t, 99cr; Twentieth Century Fox: 120b; G Webb: 77tl, 83c, 87c, 123b.

LIZARDS

Art Archive/Dagli Orti: 165tl; Aaron Bauer: 183br; Chris Brown: 167tr; Corbis: 174b; Ecoscene: 144t, 175cr; Bill Love: 131b; Chris Mattison: 136bl, 139bl, 142t, 144br, 145br, 151cl, 155b, 168, 170bl, 171b, 172t, 175t, 175cl; Natural History Museum: 130b; NHPA: 130t, 130c, 133t, 134t, 135cr, 135b, 136t, 137c, 137b, 139t, 142bl, 143b, 144bl, 145t, 146t, 149t, 149br, 151cr, 154c, 154b, 155tl, 155tr, 157tr, 157c, 158b, 159tl, 159c, 159b, 161tr, 161b, 163b, 164bl, 165tr, 166t, 167b, 169tl, 169tr, 169bl, 171tl, 171c, 174t, 175t, 175b, 176t, 178br, 179tr, 181tr, 181c, 186t; Nature Picture Library: 164t, 177tl; Papilio: 131t, 135cl, 150t; RSPCA: 185tl, 185br, 187t; Science Photo Library: 132t, 145bl, 160b; John Sullivan/Ribbit Photography: 132b, 165bl; Jane Burton/Warren Photographic: 161tl; Kim Taylor/Warren Photographic: 132c, 138t, 156, 166c, 173tr, 177tr. All other photographs supplied courtesy of Mark O'Shea.

TURTLES

Corbis: 194t, 195t, 195c, 197l, 197tr, 198b, 202t, 205tl, 205br, 206t, 207bl, 210b, 211tl, 211b, 215l, 217c, 219tl, 224b, 231br, 236t, 237c, 237b, 238, 239l, 242b, 244t, 245tl, 247bl, 247tr; Bill Love: 194b, 195b, 199tr, 201l, 205bl, 205r, 209t, 209c, 221bl, 221br, 223b, 229t, 231l, 232, 233bl, / courtesy of Marc Cantos, Burgundy Reptiles 215br, 243tr; Mary Evans Picture Library: 191tl, 199br; Chris Mattison: 191cr, 193b, 198c, 201r, 203c, 211tr, 228t, 241t, 246t; Natural History Picture Agency: 190t, 192b, 195t, 207tr, 212t, 213, 225l, 228b, 229br, 230b, 233tl, 234b; Nature Picture Library: 191tr, 193c, 196, 208, 209b, 212b, 214, 216t, 218t, 219b, 220b, 221tl, 223tr, 224t, 227t, 254r, 239r, 240b, 241b, 243tl, 243br; Mark O'Shea: 225br; Oxford Scientific Films: 190b, 191bl, 192t, 202b, 203b, 204, 219tr, 221tr, 225tr, 237t, 240t; Science Photo Library: 198t, 207tl, 210t, 218b, 246b; Tortoise Trust: 191br, 197tl, 199tl, 199bl, 203t, 206b, 207br, 215tr, 216b, 217t, 217b, 220t, 222, 223l, 226t, 227c, 227b, 229bl, 231tr, 233tr, 233br, 235, 236b, 242t, 243bl, 244b, 245tr, 245b, 247tl; Turtle Conservation Centre (Vietnam): 247b.

This edition is published by Armadillo, an imprint of Anness Publishing Ltd, 108 Great Russell Street, London WC1B 3NA; info@anness.com

www.annesspublishing.com

Anness Publishing has a picture agency outlet for images for publishing, promotions or advertising. Please visit our website www.practicalpictures.com for more information.

Publisher: Joanna Lorenz
Editors: Nicky Barber, Nicole Pearson, Laura Seber, Sarah Uttridge, Elizabeth Woodland and Joy Wotton
Consultants: Michael Chinery, Dr Richard A Griffiths, Andy and Nadine Highfield
Designers: Linda Penny, Ann Samuel, Rita Wuthrich and Simon Wilder
Illustrators: Linden Artists, Julian Baker, John Francis, Stuart Lafford, Vanessa Card and David Webb

Maps: Anthony Duke
Production Controller: Rosie Anness

PUBLISHER'S NOTE

Manufacturer: Anness Publishing Ltd, 108 Great Russell Street, London WC1B 3NA, England
For Product Tracking go to: www.annesspublishing.com/tracking
Batch: 7421-23431-1127